WHAT ARE THEY TEACHING OUR CHILDREN?

MEL AND NORMA GABLER
with JAMES C. HEFLEY

VICTOR BOOKS ®
A DIVISION OF SCRIPTURE PRESS PUBLICATIONS INC.
USA CANADA ENGLAND

Third printing, 1987

Recommended Dewey Decimal Classification: 371.32
Suggested Subject Heading: EDUCATION, TEXTBOOKS

Library of Congress Catalog Card Number: 84-52368
ISBN: 0-89693-362-8

VICTOR BOOKS
A division of SP Publications, Inc.
        Wheaton, Illinois 60187

CONTENTS

THE GABLERS OF LONGVIEW: SAINTS OR CENSORS?

by James C. Hefley, Ph.D.

Longview, Texas (pop. 62,762) could hardly be considered the crossroads of America. But it is infamous in the circles of "progressive" public education as the home of Mel and Norma Gabler—a couple who are placing their mark on the textbooks used by over 40 million American children. They've been so influential that the editors of the *1983 Britannica Book of the Year* listed them among ninety-five world notables—including Yuri Andropov, Steven Speilberg, and the Ronald Reagans—who "influenced events significantly in 1982."[1]

Coming off Interstate 20, partway between Shreveport and Dallas, you'll need good directions to find their house on pleasant, tree-lined Berry Lane. No name appears on the door, no sign hangs in a window to indicate that this is their home and headquarters. An aging 1971 Chevy, which they bought second-hand, is parked in the driveway. Not much to suggest that the couple (and a staff of eight) working inside are viewed by many as the leading critics of the billion-dollar public school textbook industry. Only when a TV crew arrives—as CBS, ABC, NBC, and French, British, and Japanese television have—is there any suggestion that something extraordinary is going on behind the curtained windows.

Mel and Norma Gabler are, without doubt, the most publicized and controversial couple in American education. Hardly anyone who has heard anything about them remains neutral. They're either hated or adored, praised or shellacked, labeled saints or censors.

"The Gablers operate the same way the Nazis, and the Klan, and Idi Amin, and the Ayatollah do," said a reporter from the *Panola (Texas) Watchman*, who had never met them personally.[2] William Murchison, associate editor of *The Dallas Morning News*, who has known the couple for over a decade, praises their "studious, effective criticism of school texts." "The Gablers," he wrote in an editorial, "believe in the goodness of America, the sanctity of the family, and the necessity for principled, upright standards of behavior."[3]

Mel Gabler admits they get some bad press. "But if a reporter will stay as long as two hours," he says, "and will look at textbooks, we usually get a good story."

One reporter who did is CBS-TV's Mike Wallace, perhaps the toughest interviewer in America. Before the "60 Minutes" crew came to Longview, Wallace read everything he could find on the couple, including the book documentary, *Textbooks on Trial*.[4] When he finally arrived to interview the Gablers, he unabashedly told Norma, "I know more about you than you know about yourself."

The next day in her living room, Norma showed Wallace a clutch of "objectionable and offensive" books. He picked out a passage in one of them and handed it to Norma. With the cameras rolling, he ordered her to "Read it."

Norma pushed the book back. "No, I won't."

"Read it!"

"No, I won't."

"Read it!"

"No, I won't."

Wallace then handed the book to Gabler staff member Sheila Haralson, who read a passage that was so obscene it could not be aired on television.

CBS titled the story, "What Johnny Can't Read." After noting on camera that educators have long controlled textbook content, Wallace observed that other groups, such as blacks, Hispanics, and feminists now want a say in determining what goes into textbooks. Then he got to Norma:

> But there is one woman down in Texas who says that if all those assorted groups can have their say about our textbooks, then she wants the views of the silent majority—her views—represented too. Her name is Norma Gabler, and she is formidable.

"The Gablers," he continues, "have conducted a kind of crusade to get parents to pay attention to what is in their children's books." Then Norma appears on the screen, voicing her concerns:

> Every time they try to clean up television, I say clean up your textbooks first, because . . . your children are a captive audience [in school]. They don't have the right to get up and walk out. Your television, you can turn the dial or you can turn it off. You don't turn off a classroom. Fifty years ago, parents wouldn't [have] put up with what's going on in the classroom today.

Wallace presents several examples of books the Gablers find "intolerable." Then Mel and Norma appear together, observing that many books minimize the accomplishments of American patriots. They "censor" such remarks as Nathan Hale's famous, "I only regret that I have but one life to lose for my country." They berate good citizenship. As Norma points out:

> To be a better citizen, they decided that you could be that by learning to apply for welfare at the age of fourteen. I suggested they give them [students] a job application, but I found out that the dirtiest word in the English language is W-O-R-K.

Wallace confronts Edward Jenkinson, then-chairman of the Committee Against Censorship of the National Council of Teachers of English; Richard Carroll, president of Allyn & Bacon, a major textbook publisher; and Thomas Murphy, vice-president of the textbook division of CBS-owned Holt, Rinehart & Winston:

WALLACE: Now, just how important are the Gablers?
JENKINSON: They probably have more influence on the use of textbooks in this country than any other two people.
CARROLL: In . . . the last ten years, they've become more and more of a force for publishers to contend with.
WALLACE: Has Murphy's publishing house ever changed materials to suit the Gablers?
MURPHY: Yes, we did. Sometimes we do change textbooks. All publishers do.

JENKINSON: I don't think that two people should have that power, that degree of influence. . . . I think that a teacher must have the right to teach so that students will have the right to know, and I believe that those two rights are guaranteed by the First Amendment.

NORMA GABLER: Now, it's strange that if they choose it, it's academic freedom; it's a right of selection. But, if we do it, it's censorship. The highest form of censorship is denying a parent's right to be heard, and who is doing that? The professionals. I call that censorship. And if you [parents] don't fight, nobody else will.

Wallace now asks Seibert Adams, an editor for Random House, to comment on a health book submitted in Texas for fourteen-year-olds. The book says orgasm can be achieved through pleasurable petting. Wallace notes that Random House withdrew this book from consideration in Texas shortly after the Gablers began to examine it. Adams replies that it was originally a college text, and was only later introduced into high schools.

WALLACE: You'll sell where it'll go.

ADAMS: Correct. . . . And the reason we do this is because the book takes no moralistic view.

WALLACE: It sure doesn't.

ADAMS: And we're proud of that.

Wallace turns to a contested fifth-grade history book.

WALLACE: After Mrs. Gabler called our attention to this history book, *Search for Freedom*, published by Macmillan Company, we looked at it more closely. . . . Not only does it devote seven pages to Marilyn Monroe—with nothing about Martha Washington—it contains no mention of Lyndon Johnson or Richard Nixon. Even the assassination of John Kennedy goes unmentioned. We wanted to find out why seven pages of Marilyn Monroe and nothing about Kennedy, Nixon, or Johnson. But the Macmillan Company simply refused to talk to us about it on camera.

The interview returns to the Gablers.

MEL GABLER: We do not want just our viewpoint presented to the students, but we feel it's unfair to have our [traditional values] viewpoint totally censored when at least half of the United States considers it favorable.[5]

NORMA GABLER: Government or history or literature, where's the balance?

WALLACE (concluding): And Norma Gabler says that too often, today's parents still don't know what's in their children's textbooks.[6]

"Sixty Minutes" was a big interview for the Gablers. But an interview with Phil Donahue, on whose show they've appeared three times, drew more mail. "Nearly 2,000 letters, with thirty-five to one *for* us," Mel recalls. "And that was on an issue where Donahue gave us a hard time."

Drop in almost anytime and you'll find Mel or Norma on the phone with a parent who's seeking help, a teacher wanting a review, or a reporter doing a feature about "censorship."

On this particular day, the hot subject being discussed in the Gabler household is a proposed change in Texas rules over how evolution should be presented in textbooks. Mel is talking to the *New York Times* and Norma is outlining a speech she will give in Indiana. Meanwhile, the copy machine, word processor, and typewriters run in the background; the Gablers' staff is preparing for the upcoming public hearings in Austin, where a new line of textbooks will be considered for use in Texas during the next six years.

Texas is the largest textbook buyer among twenty-three states which select books at the state level. As a result, a book that "passes" in Texas will be easier to sell elsewhere. One that "flunks" will be harder to get past adoption committees in other states. As publisher Fred McDougal told the *Chicago Tribune*, Texas "is a litmus test for how liberal a textbook can be."[7]

With the phone resting on his shoulder and a book in his hands, Mel looks like a retired college professor. Actually, he's a retired clerk from the Humble Pipe Line Company. A soft-spoken, methodical grandfather of five, he doesn't fit the image of the scurrilous censor the educational elitists make him out to be. And Norma, a buxom, smiling lady, looks more like the type you'd expect to see at a knitting bee. Quite often, they'll meet a teacher or reporter who'll immediately exclaim, "Why, you're not at all what I expected you to be."

CBS-TV from Dallas is at the door. They've chartered a plane and have flown over for an interview on creation and evolution. Norma treats them like old friends. "Mel will be with you in a minute. How about some iced tea?"

"No, we don't want to ban evolution," Mel is telling the *Times* reporter for the third time. "We've never said evolution shouldn't be taught. We do think it should be taught as a theory, which any honest scientist will tell you it is. No, no. Not all scientists believe in evolution. I can cite you many who don't. Several are world famous. There's Dr. Werner Von Braun, the man behind the space program. But then he's dead and maybe he won't count. Hold on, and I'll give you a list of others whom you might wish to call." The reporter doesn't have time. He has a deadline to make.

Mel and Norma have been concerned about textbooks since that day in 1961 when their sixteen-year-old son, Jim, insisted they take a look at his history book. Mel read it and couldn't believe his eyes. The book was top-heavy on enumerating the powers of the federal government, but said nothing about the rights of states or individuals. Many of the old patriots and their ringing cries were missing, such as Patrick Henry's "Give me liberty or give me death." Later, Mel and Norma compared the book to older history texts and reached a startling conclusion: History hadn't changed, but the publishers sure had changed history.

Since they were on a first-name basis with school officials in the area, Mel and Norma decided to find out how books were selected—and who selected them. The superintendent explained that each year in Austin, a State Textbook Committee, subject to approval by the State Board of Education, chose two to five books in certain subjects for certain grades on a rotating basis.

"We're bound to their list," the schoolman said. Then, almost as an afterthought, he told Mel, "If you want to have an impact, go to Austin."

To the everlasting regret of the public education cartel, the Gablers followed that bit of advice and headed for the state capital. Year after year they went. At first, they were perceived as little more than kooks or troublemakers. And because

Mel's oil company job tied him close to home in Hawkins, Texas, Norma initially had to do almost all the traveling herself. But at home, starting with the names on their Christmas card list, they worked together to mail out a newsletter. Slowly, they added the names of other people who showed an interest in this matter.

The Gablers also began to grasp progressive education's grand scheme to change America. They understood why the new history, economics, and social study texts trumpeted Big Brother government, welfarism, and a new socialistic global order, while putting down patriotism, traditional morality, and free enterprise. Simply stated, Mel and Norma realized that the Humanists in education were seeking to bring about the "social realism" which John Dewey and other ideologues had planned for America.

As Mel and Norma talked to educators and listened to "expert witnesses" whitewash the problems in school texts, they marveled that all these individuals could speak with such consonance. They could not believe a formal conspiracy existed. But it was clear that a well-defined mind-set existed which ran against the traditional beliefs of most Americans. The editors in the publishing houses, the writers of the textbooks, the salaried officials in the Texas Education Agency, and the educators in the field all had been trained under the same liberal philosophy. They spoke the same jargon, cheered for the same experimental programs, and hurled the same verbal brickbats at whoever dared to question their collective wisdom.

Even after he retired, Mel stayed at home to run the office while Norma took to the front lines. They learned to dot every "i" and cross every "t" in preparing the "Bills of Particulars" from which they were authorized to speak at textbook hearings. Slowly, but steadily, the Gablers and other concerned citizens persuaded the State Board to require more basic academic skills in textbooks, to permit more parental participation in the educational process, and to erect legal hedges against immorality, obscenity, socialism, and shoddy teaching in textbooks.

Winning respect and the right to be heard did not come easily. At a State Board of Education meeting, after Norma cited numerous errors and contradictions in several economics texts, a Board member demanded, "What are your qualifications? Why should we listen to anything you have to say?"

Taking a deep breath to maintain her composure, Norma

looked straight at the challenger. "Sir, I am a mother of three sons. I pay taxes from which these books are purchased. I vote to elect the member of this Board from my district. Can you think of three better reasons?"

He couldn't and she kept speaking. Another Board member, however, read a newspaper while several others talked aloud. Finally, the paper reader whined, "Mr. Chairman, why must we listen to this woman? We know how we're going to vote."

Chairman Ben Howell of El Paso was not amused. "As long as I'm chairman of this Board," he said, "any citizen will receive a hearing. Continue, Mrs. Gabler."

Year after year Norma continued. As the hearings became more open, statewide interest in this issue grew. But Mel and Norma fumed when they were misrepresented in the press. Mel finally asked sympathetic Longview editor Ellie Hopkins: "Why can't they get things straight? Why doesn't the press ever give our side?"

Hopkins pointed to a press release from the Texas Education Agency. "If they don't *have* your side, they can't print it."

"Could we send out a release?" Mel asked.

"Write it up and I'll see that it gets on the wires," he promised.

Learning how to send out press releases was a big step forward for the Gablers. They found that most media gave more objective coverage to their statements and sometimes would call to request additional information.

They also learned how to dramatize their objections. In 1973, Texas and the nation were shocked when the bodies of twenty-seven youngsters were uncovered in Houston and their murders charged against homosexual deviants. That also happened to be the year when the educational elite decided it was time to help the cause of homosexuals. So when Mel and Norma noticed how new psychology and sociology texts heralded homosexuality, they sent out a news release with quotes from the books. "TABOOS FALL IN SOME PROPOSED TEXTS," headlined the *Austin American-Statesman*. "NEW TEXTBOOKS OFFER BIZARRE MATERIAL," announced the *Longview Daily News*. One Longview editor declared:

> It leads one to wonder who is the sickest—the subjects about which these textbooks are written, the authors, the publishers, or those public officials who may seriously con-

sider adopting this type of trash for young students in Texas?[8]

During the hearings over these particular texts, Norma held up two of the books wrapped in brown paper and described them as "X-rated textbooks." She read quotes from each that apparently condoned homosexuality and incest. The publisher of these texts was so embarrassed that he apologized and asked the textbook committee not to recommend his books.

As their influence spread, the Gablers received invitations to speak in other states. They also hewed to a policy of dealing strictly with textbook content and avoiding personal attacks on companies and authors. Accordingly, their personal integrity never has been blackened. Their lives are an open book to friend and foe alike. Their non-profit organization operates on a shoestring budget. Neither Mel nor Norma receive any salary for their efforts. They live modestly off Mel's annuity—which was reduced when he took early retirement at age fifty-eight to devote himself to the textbook crusade.

Unfortunately, some of the Gablers' opponents do not share this couple's desire to avoid character assassination when discussing the textbook issue. Many hurl ridiculous and unsupportable charges against the Gablers. Often, the same diatribes appear in several publications almost simultaneously, indicating a parroting of hostile press releases.

Some of the most outlandish attacks have come from TV producer Norman Lear's People for the American Way (PAW), which runs on a multimillion dollar budget and has opened an office in Austin to counter the Gablers. In April 1982, PAW pictured the Gablers on the envelope of a fund-raising letter and stated inside that Mel and Norma were building a new 1.5 million dollar building to house their organization, Educational Research Analysts. This simply is not true. The Gablers operate out of their home and desperately need much more space, but not on that scale. They rent only 2,000 square feet of warehouse space for extra storage.

PAW pitched another fund appeal in a full-page newspaper ad warning of alleged threats to freedom from the Gablers, Jerry Falwell, and Phyllis Schlafly. The ad cited recent book burnings in six states—though none of the individuals PAW mentioned in the appeal ever participated in them. The Gablers were credited with banning new dictionaries in Texas "because they include words labeled 'objectionable.' " The Gablers had nothing to do with the removal of these dictionaries. They were rejected for Texas schools because they contained obscenities which were in violation of Texas education policy. PAW, whose letterhead boasts a veritable Who's Who of American liberals, further warned in the ad:

> They [the Gablers, Falwell, and Schlafly] racially segregate private schools, and want to use your tax money to do it.
> They want to weaken child abuse protections. . . .
> They want to involve the government in your decision to have children. Or not to.
> Some want all homosexuals executed.
> They want to deny you Social Security benefits, calling them inconsistent with the Bible.
> They want to keep you from going to court to protect your civil rights and personal liberties.
> In all, they want to force you to practice their particular religious beliefs. By law.[9]

On other fronts, the infamous *Hustler* magazine has referred to the Gablers in terms that bordered close to libel. And Dallas newspaper columnist Molly Ivins has called Mel and Norma "two ignorant, fear-mongering, right-wing fruitloops who have spent the past twenty years doing untold damage to public education in this state."[10]

The Gablers only can grin and bear it. But on one occasion, when they were on a TV show with a PAW representative, they at least were able to get the man to admit that PAW's charges often were less than truthful.

Whatever the damage and the falsehoods against the Gablers, the attacks show that educational ideologues and their cohorts in PAW and similar groups take the Gablers seriously. Very seriously.

"Let 'em ridicule us and have their fun," Norma declares. "With all their griping and complaining and outright lies about us, they can't get over the fact we're effective. They're squealing because they see the majority of Americans are getting fed up with the way textbooks are attacking traditional values."

Fortunately, the Gablers' work *is* being accurately documented in a number of quarters. Dr. Frank Piasecki, for example, received his Ph.D. from North Texas State University after writing a dissertation which chronicled the Gablers' decades-long efforts. (A copy of the 470-page dissertation is available from: University Microfilms, International, 300 North Zeeb Road, Ann Arbor, MI 48106.)

Likewise, supporters of the Gablers and their crusade for better textbooks appear to be growing in number. Mayor Starke Taylor of Dallas recently proclaimed "Mel and Norma Gabler Day" when the couple was speaking in his city. And Joe Murray, in his column for a Lufkin, Texas paper, made note of a couplet Mel had found in a first-grade supplementary reader that read, "I reeely lick Arithmetic. But spulling makes me very sic."[11] Murray pointed out that an instruction manual told teachers not to worry about:

> Children learning misspellings like this. . . . If they learn misspelling from this exposure, congratulate them on their linguistic sensitivities and show them an experience chart of the poem in proper spelling. They'll probably reject it in favor of the nonsensical, but you'll have made your point.

To this observation Murray added, "You'll also have made some dumb kids, linguistic sensitivities notwithstanding." He concluded: "And here's to you, Meddlin' Mel [Gabler]. I only wish there were more lick you. I reeely due."[12]

The scores of Gabler admirers come from a wide spectrum. A Brooklyn rabbi recently sent the signatures of a hundred "Jewish teachers and young professionals who applaud you," adding, "You've got these New York liberals paranoid."

True or not, Mel and Norma Gabler *have* been making some big waves. Whether you think you agree with them or not, you should at least read what they have to say about the textbooks which are being served up to the captive classes in America's public schools. What you learn might just lead you to guarantee your children a better future.

Footnotes

[1]*Britannica Book of the Year*, Encyclopaedia Britannica, Inc., 1983, p. 77.

[2]Jeff Loudy, "Setback," *Panola Watchman*, November 14, 1982. (Fortunately, after meeting the Gablers and looking at the evidence, Loudy later wrote a fair and objective article.)

[3]William Murchison, "Flames over Austin," *The Dallas*

WHAT ARE THEY TEACHING OUR CHILDREN?

Morning News, November 18, 1982, p. 16 A.
4James C. Hefley, *Textbooks on Trial*, Victor Books, 1976, hardcover, $6.95. An updated version titled *Are Textbooks Harming Your Children?* Mott Media, 1979, paperback, $3.95. Both books are available from the Gablers, P.O. Box 7518, Longview, TX 75607.
5Actually, at least 75 percent of Americans still hold to traditional values according to various surveys, including those conducted by Gallup and *Better Homes and Gardens* in anticipation of the 1980 White House Conference on Families; "The Connecticut Mutual Life Report on American Values in the '80s: The Impact of Belief," reports the same conclusion.
6CBS "60 Minutes" telecast over CBS-TV Network, June 15, 1980.
7Casey Banas, "A mother's war on textbooks," *Chicago Tribune*, August 19, 1979, sec. 1, p. 2.
8Editorial Views, "New Textbooks Offer Bizarre Material," *The Longview Daily News*, September 24, 1973.
9Ad placed in *Austin American-Statesman*, May 9, 1982, p. C7, and various other newspapers.
10Molly Ivins, "Bubba, why are we honoring two fear-mongering censors?" *Dallas Times Herald*, July 21, 1983, Sec. E, P. 1.
11*Sounds in the Wind*, Holt, Rinehart and Winston, Inc., 1974, p. 156.
12Joe Murray, "Keep on meddlin', Mel," *The Lufkin Daily News*, October 2, 1983, p. 2-C.

CHAPTER ONE

TEXTBOOKS HAVE CHANGED— OR HAVEN'T YOU NOTICED?

Your ten-year-old daughter is going to her girlfriend's house. "Be home by eight, Honey," you tell her as she starts to leave.

She keeps walking toward the door, apparently oblivious to your instruction.

"Didn't you hear me?" you repeat as she leaves the house. "Be home at eight."

She whirls around and snaps back, "I'll be home when I'm ready."

You take a deep breath to hold your temper in check. "I said, you are to be home at eight, young lady!"

"And, I say, Mother, I'm big enough to decide when I want to come home!"

It was behavior like that from their ten- and twelve-year-old daughters that alarmed Geri and her architect husband, Jim. For at least a month their girls had been sassy and rebellious. They had to get to the bottom of this.

"Maybe it's us," Jim suggested. "Maybe we haven't been spending enough time with them. Maybe we haven't paid enough attention to their interests."

So during the next several weeks, Geri and Jim carefully monitored their own actions and made special efforts to get closer to their children. They observed a little improvement, but not much.

"Could it be television?" Jim wondered. They kept a close eye on the girls' viewing habits, but concluded that TV was not as powerful an influence as they had thought.

"We don't know their Sunday School teacher very well," Geri noted. They checked there and with leaders of the girls' youth group. They found no reason to suspect their daughters' negative attitudes were coming from the church.

The kids kept talking back, acting as if they already were adults who didn't need to observe any rules of the home. Jim and Geri even called several parents in the neighborhood who had children around the same ages as their daughters. A number of these parents admitted their children also had become rebellious.

Suddenly the light dawned for Geri. *You dummy!* she told herself. *Who has your kids more than anyone else? The school!*

Geri and Jim's kids always had made good grades and seldom asked for parental help with homework. As a result, Geri never had really read any of their books. When she mentioned this to Jim, he replied, "I haven't either. Why don't you check out some of the stuff they've been exposed to in school?"

Geri thought that would be easy. She got an appointment with a teacher she had met at PTA. The teacher referred her to the principal, he to the superintendent, and she ended up—on her third trip to the school—facing four unsmiling people, including the curriculum director. They told her she could look at her daughters' books only when the teachers allowed the children to take them home. "And that isn't too often," the principal said. "It's our policy to keep the materials here. So many kids lose them and the expense adds up."

Geri and Jim almost had to call a meeting of the school board, but they finally managed to get a stack of textbooks. Geri read them line by line and showed some of the passages to Jim. Disgusted and depressed by what they found, the couple was at a loss about what to do next. Finally, when they were talking about the books at dinner with a group of friends, someone brought up our names and suggested they call us.

Geri voiced their main complaints to us: the texts included exercises requiring students to list personal information about themselves and their parents; encouraged questioning of parental authority; suggested students form their own values, independent of the home; featured stories about rebellion and violence among children; etc., etc., etc.

We listened and had an assistant mail our reviews of some of the books Geri listed. "Thank you, thank you, thank you," Geri said. "I'm sure I'll be back in touch. Jim and I are determined to do something about this awful stuff in our kids' books."

Geri and Jim persisted. They organized a parents' group. They documented their complaints before members of the local school board. They made some headway.

We talked on the phone with them at least a dozen times. On one occasion, Jim said, "If you had told me a year ago about the content of students' books, I would have hung up in your ear or just said, 'Yeah, yeah,' and considered you a nut. I couldn't have conceived what was going on."

A Widespread Problem

We've heard from hundreds of upset parents like Geri and Jim. Not all are as persistent or successful. They're upset about different things. One mother sputtered that she saw her six-year-old daughter groaning and twisting her pelvis one day. "Where did you learn that?" the mother asked.

"Oh, in school today," the child answered. "We saw a film of a woman having a baby. Then we all pretended we were giving birth."

Another mother reported, "They took my kindergartener with her class to the funeral home without asking me. They call it 'death education.' "

Still another sobbed, "My son killed himself. We found pages of school notes in his pocket about death and suicide. Just reading this horrible stuff would make you want to do away with yourself."

We've heard from parents, teachers, and other concerned people in every state in the U.S., and over twenty-five foreign countries. This is not a local problem. Norma found similar problems in Australia and New Zealand. A French TV crew who filmed in our home said they are having the same problem. French textbooks are not conveying the values held by the general public. Later, a Japanese TV crew in our home confirmed the same situation exists in Japan.

Our experience before getting involved in this issue was fairly similar to that of other parents. For many years we trusted the school and its curriculum. Then we went through an uneasy period. "It looks sometimes as if our kids are *un*learning," Norma mentioned a number of times. But we didn't connect this with their textbooks until our son, Jim, insisted we take a close look at his history book.

That set us off. We looked at other textbooks and really became alarmed. We saw that textbooks had drastically changed for the worse since we were in school in the 1920s and '30s.

Everybody who reviews and compares new and old textbooks recognizes this change. Every study we've seen or heard about has documented a parallel drop in student test scores and literacy. Despite the educational establishment's denials, the public perception is that our schools are in crisis. Over 80 percent of the 130,000 persons who responded to a survey by *Family Weekly* said today's schools are inadequately preparing children for the future, and that 40 to 50 percent of all high school graduates are functionally illiterate.[1] Former-Senator George McGovern, a longtime defender of the liberal educational establishment, called this situation "alarming" and proposed a national "Commission on Literacy."[2]

A reporter for a major national magazine once came to our home for an interview. We wondered how he would treat us. We needn't have. He did a fair and accurate story. You see, his daughter had come to him a few nights before and said, "My friend is about to lose her job because she doesn't know how to make change. Would you teach her how?" He agreed and spent an hour helping this eighteen-year-old high school graduate learn a skill she should have mastered in the third grade. Naturally, he was ready to listen when he came to interview us.

The Results of Poor Textbooks

As former-Secretary of Education Terrell Bell put it, textbooks have been "dumbed down"—they've been made less difficult because students can't handle harder material. If you don't believe it, ask any principal how many of his seniors could answer at least six of these test questions:

(1) In what state and on what waters are the following: Chicago, Duluth, Cleveland, and Buffalo? State an important fact about each.
(2) What causes the change from day to night, and from summer to winter?
(3) What is meant by inflection? What parts of speech are inflected?
(4) Write a model business letter of not more than 40 words.

(5) A rope 500 feet long is stretched from the top of a tower and reaches the ground 300 feet from the base of the tower; how high is the tower?

(6) Write a brief biography of *Evangeline*.

(7) Give the structure of a muscle and the spinal cord.

(8) Define arteries, veins, capillaries, and pulse.

These questions were selected from a test given in Indiana for students desiring *entry* to high school in 1911.[3]

You don't have to guess the results of a similar test given to high school seniors today. *The Chattanooga Times*, for example, polled seniors in six local high schools and found that one-third couldn't name the mayor of their city or the Vice-President of the United States.[4]

Academic ineptness isn't the only problem plaguing kids entering today's work force. Employers complain about rotten attitudes. In another newspaper feature, Geraldine Sharpe, a personnel manager for the General Services Administration, reports that bad work attitudes cause more secretarial firings than poor performance. "Not only do they not accept responsibility," she says, "they just don't feel any obligation to stick with a job."[5]

National concern also has arisen over the appalling rise in pregnancies, drug use, assaults, and incidents of thievery and vandalism among teenagers. Nearly a third of the babies born to white teenage girls and 83 percent born to black teens are illegitimate. And there are five abortions for every three live births.[6]

Robberies in schools jumped 113 percent in just three years during the past decade. Assault and battery jumped 58 percent during the 1970s. Sex offenses climbed 72 percent, paralleling the increase in sex education courses. Tens of thousands of teachers are attacked every year.[7]

Perhaps the most graphic means by which to highlight these alarming trends is to contrast them with the top offenses of public school students in 1940:

(1) Talking

(2) Chewing gum

(3) Running in the halls

(4) Wearing improper clothing

(5) Making noise

(6) Not putting paper in wastebaskets

(7) Getting out of turn in line

Compare that list to the top offenses of students forty years later:

(1) Rape	(11) Absenteeism
(2) Robbery	(12) Vandalism
(3) Assault	(13) Murder
(4) Personal theft	(14) Extortion
(5) Burglary	(15) Gang warfare
(6) Drug abuse	(16) Pregnancies
(7) Arson	(17) Abortions
(8) Bombings	(18) Suicide
(9) Alcohol abuse	(19) Venereal disease
(10) Carrying of weapons	(20) Lying and cheating*

Blame the family, TV, movies, capitalism, Congress, the President, and low teacher salaries for these problems, say defensive educators. Blame anything and anyone. But don't blame what kids are being taught in school!

We don't pretend to assume that teaching materials are wholly at fault. The commercial mass media have been a terrible influence on our young people. Divorce, absentee fathers, single working mothers, unemployed parents, and poverty certainly have contributed. But public miseducation and textbooks which undermine parental and religious authority deserve much of the blame, both directly and indirectly. Poor education dooms many youngsters to menial, low-paying jobs or unemployment. Perverted "values education"—which sanctions immorality—can tear families apart.

The Struggle Ahead

It's foolish to underestimate the power of textbooks on what students study. Seventy-five percent of students' classroom time and 90 percent of homework time is spent with textbook materials. To quote the *State Education Review:* "Obviously, any attempt to improve education must involve taking a look at textbooks and their powerful role in education."[9]

Parents usually don't know how much textbooks have changed for the worse. Why? Because they haven't bothered to look. At first, we refused to believe our son when he told us his textbook was off base. When we finally *did* look at it, we could hardly believe what we were seeing. The more we read, the angrier we became.

We're still deeply concerned, but we're no longer puzzled. We were fooled a long time because we blindly trusted the educational establishment. We have our eyes open now and have been trying to educate school officials and the public about bad textbooks for over two decades.

We see the big picture and they know it. We understand the philosophy, ideology, and goals of so-called "progressive" education. We know how much the content of many textbooks differs from traditional morality, from what most parents think is in these books. We've found that when we show textbooks to parents, many become angry and want to do something. We believe that if we just can make enough people aware, this terrible trend eventually will be reversed. That's why we've written this book. That's why we're giving our strength and time and home every day of the year without salary. That's why we've made the improvement of school curriculum a major priority for the rest of our lives.

Footnotes

[1] Mary Long, "The Crisis in Our Schools," *Family Weekly*, October 19, 1980, pp. 4, 6.
[2] *Congressional Record*, vol. 125, no. 53, May 2, 1979, p. 1 of McGovern reprint.
[3] William H. Bell, "What Farm Kids Knew in 1911," *Wall Street Journal*, July 25, 1983.
[4] Mark Kennedy and Julie Johnston, "High school seniors: What they know—and what they don't know," *The Chattanooga Times*, March 8, 1984, p. C1.
[5] Mark Kennedy, "Many in entry-level jobs project 'bad attitudes,' personnel manager says," *The Chattanooga Times*, February 9, 1984, p. B1.
[6] "Black and White, Unwed All Over," *Time*, November 9, 1981, p. 67.
[7] Information from the International Association of School Security Directors.
[8] Private research conducted by Cullen Davis, P.O. Box 1224, Ft. Worth, TX 76101.
[9] *State Education Review*, 1983, special issue 2, Educ. Comm. of the States, Denver, CO 80295, p. 4, col. 1.

CHAPTER TWO

HOW PUBLIC SCHOOL CURRICULUM GOT THE WAY IT IS

Our class in the history of public education will now come to order.

Question: When and how did public education get started?

Answer: You may be surprised to learn that secular public education under state auspices in the United States is less than 150 years old. In 1837 the Massachusetts State Legislature voted to form America's first State Board of Public Instruction.

Community church-related schools had existed in America for 230 years before that time. The first school was established in 1607 at the Jamestown colony in Virginia. Its teacher was the Reverend Patrick Copeland, chaplain of a British ship which brought colonists to the New World. He taught the Jamestown children "religion, civility of life, and humane learning."[1]

Dutch Protestants established the first free school in New Netherland (later named New York) in 1633. New England Puritans established a school system in 1647 requiring each community in the Massachusetts Bay Colony to hire a schoolmaster in each township of fifty or more families. The purpose of these schools was to thwart "that old deluder, Satan, to keep men from knowledge of ye Scriptures."[2]

Church-related community schools, patterned after mother denominations in Europe, soon sprang up in other colonies. All taught the Bible and would be labeled parochial or Christian schools today.

Institutions of higher education in America—including Yale,

24

Harvard, Brown, and Dartmouth—also were established by church groups.

The idea of secular public education actually began in the early 1800s. Horace Mann, then-president of the Massachusetts State Senate, and Massachusetts Governor Edward Everett were followers of Germany's new Hegelian philosophy, which claimed nothing was absolute and that man's ideas were superior to biblical principles. Mann, Everett, and the newly appointed Unitarian administration of Harvard also favored the humanistic public schools then operating in the German state of Prussia. They were successful in pushing secular education laws through the Massachusetts Legislature in 1837. Other state legislatures followed suit.

Question: Did textbooks, then, become secular?

Answer: This did not happen until well into the twentieth century. Texts before the Revolutionary War taught the doctrine of church sponsors. The famed *New England Primer* was avowedly Calvinistic and taught children the alphabet by theological verses beginning, "In Adam's fall, we sinned all." The textbooks were virtual catechisms.

After Independence, school texts centered on beliefs common to all major Protestant denominations in America. Noah Webster, a Congregational choir director, began his popular *Blueback Speller* with this prayer:

No man may put off the law of God.
My joy is in His law all the day.
O may I not go in the way of sin.
Let me not go in the way of ill men.

Webster also wove biblical teachings into his first dictionary. Two examples:

Hope: A well-founded scriptural *hope* is, in our religion, the source of ineffable happiness.
Love: The Christian *loves* his Bible. If our hearts are right, we *love* God above all things.[3]

Bible-oriented textbooks continued in the schools even after various state legislatures took control of education, though sectarian teaching was prohibited. Most popular were the *McGuffey's Readers*, which ultimately sold 122 million copies. McGuffey, a fervent frontier preacher, taught biblical moral virtues through entertaining "character" stories. Public schools continued to be so Protestant in nature that immigrant Catholics felt compelled to start their own parochial schools in the 1890s.

Question: Weren't these activities in violation of the First Amendment?

Answer: Look closely at the wording of the First Amendment in regard to religion: "Congress shall make no law respecting an *establishment* of religion, or *prohibiting the free exercise thereof*" (our emphasis). "Establishment" to the Founders—and to American political and judicial leaders for almost two centuries—meant organizing a government religious denomination. The Founders wisely saw that the Federal government and denominational institutions must be separated. They never intended, however, for religion and the state to have absolutely no connection.

The phrase "separation of church and state," which is cited so frequently today, is *not* in the Constitution or the First Amendment. It was used only in Thomas Jefferson's letter to the Danbury Baptist Association of Connecticut. Multitudes of Americans have been led falsely to believe that the Constitution separates government and Judeo-Christian morality. Not even the most liberal Supreme Court ruling has ever claimed this.

Not until the early 1960s did the Supreme Court order "official" prayer and Bible reading banned from school. This was done on grounds that the school was officially "respecting an establishment of religion." Many polls indicate that most Americans still disagree with this interpretation.

Question: Who was most instrumental in secularizing textbooks?

Answer: John Dewey, a philosophy professor at Columbia University and the University of Chicago. A declared atheist who sometimes used religious terminology, Dewey was a Hegelian, holding that truth always is in process; it never is eternally fixed. Morals changed, he believed, as society changed. Students should, therefore, be taught to adjust socially and ethically to change as it occurs. Change and adjust, change and adjust. That was Dewey's theme.

Dewey was the first president of the American Humanist Association and a signer of Humanist Manifesto I in 1933. To understand the philosophy and goals of modern "progressive" education, you need only to ponder the opening paragraphs of Humanist Manifesto I:

The time has come for widespread recognition of the radical changes in religious beliefs throughout the modern world. The time is past for mere revision of traditional attitudes. Science and economic change have disrupted the old beliefs. Religions the world over are under the necessity of coming to terms with new conditions created by a vastly increased knowledge and experience. In every field of human activity, the vital movement is now in the direction of a candid and explicit humanism. In order that religious humanism may be better understood we, the undersigned, desire to make certain affirmations which we believe the facts of our contemporary life demonstrate.

There is great danger of a final, and we believe fatal, identification of the word *religion* with doctrines and methods which have lost their significance and which are powerless to solve the problem of human living in the Twentieth Century. . . .

While this age does owe a vast debt to traditional religions, it is nonetheless obvious that any religion that can hope to be a synthesizing and dynamic force for today must be shaped for the needs of this age. To establish such a religion is a major necessity of the present. It is a responsibility which rests upon this generation. We therefore affirm the following:
First: Religious humanists regard the universe as self-existing and not created.
Second: Humanism believes that man is a part of nature and that he has emerged as the result of a continuous process. . . .
Sixth: We are convinced that the time has passed for theism. . . .
Seventh: Religion consists of those actions, purposes, and experiences which are humanly significant. Nothing human is alien to the religious. . . . The distinction between the sacred and the secular can no longer be maintained.[4]

Question: Who were Dewey's chief allies?
Answer: A great host of Americans knowingly—and unknow-

ingly—supported the "father" of "progressive" education. Liberal theologians, for example, used the methods of German "higher criticism" to attack the authority and authenticity of the Bible. American universities advocated Darwin's theory of evolution. Within so-called intellectual circles it became fashionable to reject theism and the Bible for the "natural" belief that man must be his own savior. This set the stage for Humanists to seize the helm in public education.

Dewey's most vocal support, however, came from professors in the universities which trained future educators. Later, the National Education Association (NEA) joined in, urging that students be conditioned to change and adjust, and their behavior modified, just as rats are trained in stimulus-response experiments. Said the NEA's Department of Superintendence in 1932:

> Conditioning is therefore a process which may be employed by the teacher to build up attitudes in the child and predispose him to the actions by which these attitudes are expressed.[5]

The NEA further stated that:

> Agencies such as the school must assume responsibilities which in the past have rested upon the home and community.[6]

Question: How was "progressive" education influenced by foreign ideologies other than Darwinism, Hegelianism, and German higher criticism?

Answer: The Soviet Marxist system held a great allure for Dewey and his Humanist friends. They were among many naive American intellectuals in the 1930s who became enraptured with reports flowing from Stalin's propaganda machine. Some actually joined the American Communist Party, though Dewey is not known to have done so. After Stalin's purges and his murder of millions of Russian citizens became publicly known, most of these gullible Americans renounced any formal Communist ties. But many continued to believe that the Marxist-socialist model was "better" for the masses than American constitutional liberty and private property.

Dewey and his colleagues' infatuation with Marxism is a fact of history that can be documented in the history section of any university library. It is not a figment of the imagination of anti-Communists. Scores of American "progressive" educators trooped to Russia in the early 1930s and returned gushing with praise for social advances wrought by Marxism. They praised Lenin and Stalin for giving Soviet citizens universal suffrage, civil liberties, the right to employment, to free education, to free medical care, and to material security in old age.

American progressive educators wanted American education to follow the "progressive" Stalinist model. So at the 1934 session of the NEA's Department of Superintendence, Willard E. Givens reported from a committee that:

> Many drastic changes must be made. A dying laissez-faire must be completely destroyed and all of us, including the "owners," must be subjected to a large degree of social control. A large section of our discussion group maintains that . . . the credit agencies, the basic industries and utilities cannot be centrally planned and operated under private ownership.

Givens and his associates recommended a plan for taking over these organizations and operating them at full capacity as a unified national system in the interest of all the people.[7]

Three years later NEA leaders flatly declared:

> The present capitalistic and nationalistic social system has been supplanted in but one place—Russia—and that change was effected by revolution. Hence the verdict of history would seem to indicate that we are likely to have to depend upon revolution for social change of an important and far-reaching character.[8]

Many more statements of this view are on record. More incriminating is a study of American textbooks, particularly history and economics texts published since the 1930s. We, and others, have cited hundreds of examples of pro-Marxist and pro-socialist propaganda in school books. Some Texas Board of Education members and leading newspaper editors in our state have recognized this slant and roundly lectured publishers for carrying the pro-socialist line. This topic will be further explained in chapter 4. Let us say at this point, however, so that none will fail to understand: We are not on a witch-hunt against any educator, author, or publisher. But we *will* point out the existence of collectivistic, pro-Marxist propaganda in textbooks.

Question: The great majority of Americans always have believed in God as revealed in the Bible. Where were the Protestant, Catholic, and Jewish leaders when secularists were changing our textbooks?

Answer: Catholics built parochial schools. Jews believed their children would suffer less discrimination in a secular system. Protestants divided.

Liberal Protestants and "social gospelers" supported the secularization of education. Many Baptists, who were not necessarily liberal, were duped by the false belief that biblical teaching and prayer in schools violated the First Amendment.

At this time, unfortunately, conservative Protestants also were caught up in a prophecy "fever." Many thought the second coming of Christ was close at hand; consequently, instead of trying to influence American political and social life, they concentrated solely on evangelism, holy personal living, and Bible study. While the liberals and Humanists were changing American education, the conservative Protestants were holding great evangelistic rallies and Bible conferences. It was not until after World War II that conservative, Bible-believing Christians realized their mistake in not having used their influence to affect education.

During this "cop-out period," future educators were being trained by Humanist professors in teachers' colleges. These educators, in turn, joined the staffs of smaller colleges, public school systems, state and federal education agencies, and textbook publishers. A bias toward secular humanism thus developed within the broad structure of education. The education fraternity became snobbish toward parents and traditional values. They became hostile and adversarial ("We educators know what's best for your children"). It became popular among educators to ignore God, the Bible, the supernatural, the traditional family, and to regard majority opinion as "unprogressive."

Question: Where are we now?

Answer: Thankfully, the Judeo-Christian mainstream is awakening to the Humanist minority's takeover of public school curriculum. But, as we shall show in succeeding chapters, the Humanists have made heavy inroads into the books which our children must study.

Our experience has shown that humanistic educators are ripe for counterattack. For the first time in several generations they are on the defensive, as their ideological bankruptcy has become obvious. But their material resources still are far greater than ours. Our leading opponent, for example, raised over $4 million in one year to combat the return of traditional values to our society. A sizable portion of this amount is being used to counter our struggles against bad textbooks in Texas. Humanists also command a good portion of the billions in funds allocated by state and federal educational agencies, in which they are well entrenched. By contrast, the annual budget of our small nonprofit, tax-exempt corporation, Educational Research Analysts, is about $130,000.

But we are not disheartened. At least 200 parent groups across the country are battling for better textbooks. Ministers, priests, and rabbis who once would never have thought of criticizing education are speaking out. Many business leaders, political officeholders, and some educators are joining them.

Our greatest challenge is to awaken the multitudes who share the morals and values under attack in today's curriculum. As a pastor from Maine recently wrote us: "I find that the average parent, even a Christian, is totally unaware of what is being taught to children in public schools across this land."

Question: What are the vital issues at stake?

Answer: Do parents have the primary right—preeminent over the school and state—to control the education of their children? Or do educators—who hold values that differ from parents—have the right to determine the spiritual, political, and economic outlook of students?

Should schools teach knowledge, skills, and the heritage of home, church, and nation? Or should they teach students that knowledge is what is personally "relevant" to them?

Do educators have the right to use our children as guinea pigs in behavior modification experiments? Should our children be under the direction of ideologues hostile to Judeo-Christian values and American constitutional liberty?

The basic issue is simple: Which principles will shape the minds of our children? Those which uphold family, morality, freedom, individuality, and free enterprise; or those which advocate atheism, evolution, secularism, and a collectivism in which an elite governs and regulates religion, parenthood, education, property, and the lifestyle of all members of society?

If we seem to be coming on too strongly, weigh the evidence we present in the upcoming chapters. Check our sources. Review the books now being set before your children. Research the principles, methods, and goals of humanistic education. Then decide if you should continue to sit on the sidelines, or join the growing number of concerned Americans who are trying to free our schools and curriculum from humanist control.

Footnotes

[1]*American Education: The Colonial Experience 1607-1783*, Harper & Row, 1970.
[2]James C. Hefley, *America: One Nation under God*, Victor Books, 1975, pp. 77-78.
[3]*Ibid.*, p. 80.
[4]*Humanist Manifesto I*, Prometheus Books, 1973, pp. 7-9.
[5]*Tenth Yearbook*, National Educational Association, Department of Superintendence. Cited in Alan Stang, "The NEA: Dictatorship of the Educariat," *American Opinion*, March 1972, reprint p. 5.
[6]*Ibid.*
[7]*Thirteenth Yearbook*, National Education Association, Department of Superintendence. Cited in Stang, "Dictatorship," reprint p. 5.
[8]*Fifteenth Yearbook*, National Education Association, Department of Superintendence. Cited in Stang, "Dictatorship," reprint p. 5.

RELIGION IS BACK IN SCHOOL

Would it shock you to know that a "new" religion is being taught in textbooks today—a religion that is hostile to the Judeo-Christian principles upon which American liberty is founded?

To indoctrinate our children in this "new" religion, the educational establishment first must rid education of sympathy for the ethics of the great majority of Americans, past and present. They must alienate our children from the morals and faith of their fathers and mothers.

Here are some illustrations of what is happening.

Joan Podchernikoff of Rohnert Park, California objected to a "how-to" book on masturbation which her ten-year-old daughter brought home from school. Joan and her husband felt the book undermined the moral values they were trying to instill in their children. When Joan went to file a complaint, the principal told her his secretary should have caught the troublesome passages when she screened the book to make sure there were no references to God![1]

We hear stories like this from all across the country. An Ohio parent told us recently that the American Civil Liberties Union (ACLU) was suing her school board over the placement of Gideon New Testaments in the fifth grade.

"The school is so upset over the suit," she said, "that it's considering censoring Nativity scenes, Christmas plays and carols, and anything else that pertains to God."

Our own town of Longview hasn't escaped this problem. Recently, a group of local Gideons asked if they could give out free New Testaments in a middle school. School officials denied them entry but said they could park out on the street; any child who wanted a New Testament could go and get one. Not a single student came out.

Miami schools even have stopped scheduling spring break around Easter for fear of "advancing religion." Does this mean they'll move winter vacation from December to January to avoid any association with Christmas?

As we've seen in earlier chapters, the anti-God bandwagon already was rolling when the Supreme Court banned Bible reading and state-prepared prayers from public schools in 1962 and 1963. Accordingly, some educators used these rulings as an excuse to clean Bibles out of school libraries. In Kanawha County, West Virginia, school officials had all Bibles removed from the public schools and dumped in an incinerator. An upset janitor retrieved one and gave it to Board of Education member Alice Moore. Moore subsequently held the charred Bible before TV cameras and recalled that the district previously had burned textbooks which were considered outdated.

"Why were the Bibles removed from the classrooms?" she asked. "Were they also outdated? We who protest bad textbooks are accused of book burning and Nazi tactics, but we're not the *real* book burners."[2]

Are Americans a Religious People?

There's more—much more—to this movement against the Judeo-Christian faith than banning Bibles from classrooms and libraries. Publishers consistently censor or distort the role of the Bible and Christianity in the founding and development of America. Yet in doing so, they are ignoring numerous legal decisions that have reaffirmed America's Christian heritage.

In 1892, for example, the Supreme Court made an exhaustive study of the connections between Christianity and U.S. history. The Court concluded that we are "a religious people" and the United States is a "Christian nation."[3]

In 1932, Justice George Sutherland looked at the 1892 decision and reiterated the belief that we are a "Christian people."[4] In 1952, Justice William O. Douglas, who was not known to possess a traditional faith, affirmed in *Zorach v. Clauson:* "We are a religious people whose institutions presuppose a Supreme Being."[5]

Unfortunately, textbook publishers don't seem to realize this.

We've searched textbooks—in vain—for quotations from such founding fathers as John Adams, who observed the settlement of America "with reverence and wonder, as the opening of a grand scheme and design in Providence for the illumination of the ignorant, and the emancipation of the slavish part of mankind all over the earth."[6]

Most history texts omit the Pilgrims' famous "Mayflower Compact," which said, in part:

> We are knit together in a body in a strict and sacred bond and covenant of the Lord, of the violation whereof we make great conscience, and by virtue whereof we do hold ourselves strictly tied to all care of each other's good, and of the whole by every one, and so mutually.[7]

Many books no longer tell the story of the first Thanksgiving. Most delete "The Fundamental Orders of Connecticut," in which Pastor Thomas Hooker called for an "orderly and decent government according to God." This first state constitution later became the prototype for the Constitution of the United States.[8]

Today's textbooks, almost without fail, censor William Penn's desire to establish Pennsylvania as a "holy experiment" in religious and political freedom. One text discusses Penn's secretary, James Logan, for five pages, while virtually ignoring the great Quaker leader.[9]

The "new histories" never tell students that on the same day Congress adopted the First Amendment, its members also voted to install congressional chaplains and official days of thanksgiving and prayer. If Congress had meant to separate this nation from the God of the Bible, it surely would not have acted in such a manner.

All the "new histories" we've seen censor Benjamin Franklin's request for prayer when the Constitutional Convention had reached a crippling impasse. Addressing the President of the Convention, Franklin said:

> We have been assured, Sir, in the Sacred Writings, that "Except the Lord build the house, they labor in vain that build it." I firmly believe this; and I also believe that without His concurring aid, we shall succeed in this political building no better than the builders of Babel; we shall

be divided in our little partial local interests, our projects will be confounded, and we ourselves shall become a reproach and a byword down to future ages. And what is worse, mankind may hereafter, from this unfortunate instance, despair of establishing Government by human wisdom and leave it to chance, war, or conquest. I therefore beg leave to move: That henceforth, prayers imploring the assistance of Heaven, and its blessings on our deliberations, be held in this Assembly every morning before we proceed to business, and that one or more of the clergy of this city be requested to officiate in that service.[10]

After the Convention paused for prayer, goodwill and conciliation prevailed. The Constitution was completed and sent to the states for ratification.

The subject of Franklin's prayer arose at a Texas textbook hearing. Norma noted that a certain text omitted the fact that the Constitutional Convention reached agreement only after Franklin insisted on prayer.[11] The publisher replied that any mention of Franklin's request for prayer could "be objected to on a number of constitutional and historical grounds."[12]

The Attack on Christianity

In light of such examples, it's abundantly clear that publishers don't provide students with historical facts about the influence of the Bible and Christianity upon our nation. Yet they *do* print books attacking our faith.

How's this for conveying the false idea that Christianity is out of date:

For a very few, religion can still provide a special sense of embracing belonging and selfhood; but for most, religion is but a Sunday meeting house and nursery school, and a recreation center, which cannot adequately define the entire person.[13]

Reflect on this gem of advice to impressionable young people:

It is thought-provoking to carry creativity training to its ultimate extreme, as at least one author has done. He suggests that if we wanted to truly induce completely creative thinking, we should teach children to question the Ten Commandments, patriotism, the two-party system, monogamy, and the laws against incest.[14]

In one brief, packaged statement, this text manages to plant seeds of doubt in the minds of youthful students concerning their moral, social, religious, and political values.

The 1974 West Virginia protests—which demanded better textbooks—stemmed in part from the books' attacks on Christianity. Professor George Hillocks, Jr. of the University of Chicago noted this in an article for an educational journal:

> Sometimes the deprecations of Christianity which the protesters point out are explicit. More often they are implicit and, therefore, even more dangerous: Sunday School depicted as a tedious bore, a minister characterized as self-righteous, photographs of churches in obvious states of decay and collapse. The inclusion of "god," "goddamn," "Christ," and related euphemisms is interpreted as a tacit approval of breaking the third commandment. The presentation of evolution as established fact is taken as a clear denial of biblical validity. Evidence of what the protesters call "situation ethics" (asking youngsters if it is ever right to steal or lie, and, if so, under what conditions) is interpreted as a denial of absolute values and, therefore, of "an ultimate cause" and a God who provides "a guarantee of human values."[15]

Incidentally, Professor Hillocks had been asked to revise a textbook series for the Scott, Foresman Company (a major textbook publisher) before speaking on the West Virginia protest to the National Council of Teachers of English. After voicing his opinions, a Scott, Foresman vice-president contacted Hillocks and informed him he need not attend the planning meetings for the revision. "You made them (the English teachers) think that perhaps the protesters were right," the vice-president said.[16]

Inadequate, humanistic distortions of Bible history further undermine students' faith. Once, at a textbook hearing, the Rev. Charles A. Clough—an MIT graduate—objected to a text's humanistic interpretation of early Hebrew history.[17] In defense, the publisher cited ten "scholarly" sources—all liberal—which the author had used in writing this history.[18] Clough pointed out that only *four* of the persons on the list were recognized scholars; moreover, the author had ignored conservative Jewish and Christian scholarship and the latest and best archeological discoveries in assembling his conclusions.

Despite such perceptive criticisms, Humanist interpretations of biblical events persist. Here is what one text says about Moses leading the Hebrews across the Red Sea:

> Moses may have led them across some shallow swamps and into the Sinai (SIGH-nigh) desert. The Hebrews called these swamps the "Sea of Reeds" because of the tall grass that grew in them. It may be that the Sea of Reeds was later called the Red Sea by mistake.[19]

This is what the Bible says about that same incident:

> Then Moses stretched out his hand over the sea; and the Lord swept the sea back by a strong east wind all night, and turned the sea into dry land, so the waters were divided. And the sons of Israel went through the midst of the sea on the dry land, and the waters were like a wall to them on their right hand and on their left.[20]

The publisher *could* have quoted the Bible. Or he *could* have balanced the narrative by citing scholars who believe in the miracle. But we'd never hold our breath waiting for any publisher to do so.

By placing Bible miracle stories under the heading of "mythology," students' faith also is attacked. Take this example from a psychology text:

> A great many myths deal with the idea of rebirth. Jesus, Dionysus, Odin, and many other traditional figures are represented as having died, after which they were reborn, or arose from the dead.[21]

The biblical account of the Fall also is handled as a myth:

> On the other hand, myths may give a picture of the world as having fallen from a perfect state. The evil of the world, according to these traditions, resulted from man's failure to obey the will of God, and it is only by following the will of God that the world can be restored to its proper state. This is essentially the mythological standpoint of Christianity, Judaism, Islam, and many other religions.[22]

The book just quoted from is geared for high school students. A more subtle way of mythologizing the Fall is found in an

38

elementary English text. Here the children are directed to create their own myths:

> One way to make up a myth is to think of a question like . . . *Why do men have pain?* Now, imagine a time when man did not have pain. Pretend that the first men on earth went around without ever feeling pain. Next imagine that some kind of god walked among men and something happened. Maybe a man did something bad or made a bad mistake. Because of this the god punished men, giving them pain for the rest of their days.[23]

We've made our point. The Bible and Christianity no longer are respected in public school curriculum. Instead, the beliefs of many parents are ridiculed and assaulted.

We're not asking for in-school catechisms and Bible lessons. But we *do* protest our children's textbooks being used as channels for attacks on biblical beliefs and Judeo-Christian morals. This clearly violates the First Amendment.

Deadly Games

The problem doesn't end here. Modern textbooks indoctrinate our children in tenets of nonbiblical religions.

Curriculum in world history studies deals with Buddhism and Hinduism, for example. We do not object to teaching facts *about* these religions. We do object to teaching—as fact—the relativistic premise that all religions are products of human imagination. We also protest the use of role playing techniques in teaching about other religions. One world cultures book, for example, includes an assignment where the children pretend they are Hindus for several days.[24]

Some texts even involve students in occult practices. Examples of this phenomenon are legion. The text or teacher may require students to perform research on the occult. An ex-warlock, who once worked in a school for witches and warlocks in North Carolina, came home to East Texas and was shocked when his thirteen-year-old nephew showed him a book from the Gladewater Middle School library. Entitled *Curses, Hexes and Spells*, the book detailed incantations and included a section on "everyday curses."

We thought we had seen it all until we came across a "witch license application" in a sixth-grade skills handbook. After describing the bizarre things witches do, the book states:

Suppose that you wanted to pursue a career as a witch. These days you might have to apply for a license and perhaps even join a witches' union. In any case, by filling out an application your aptitude for witchcraft could be evaluated.[25]

The application includes such questions as: "What words would you use to cast a spell?" and "What is your favorite formula for a witches' brew?"[26]

If the calls and letters we receive are any indication, the greatest challenge from the occult—in and out of school—is the macabre and violent fantasy game, "Dungeons and Dragons." We've heard stories of children undergoing personality changes and becoming addicted to this game's fantasy land of witches and clerics, demons and deities, dragons and dwarfs. We also know that numerous young people who have played Dungeons and Dragons have become suicide victims.

D & D is a role-playing fantasy game presided over by a "dungeon master" who creates an imaginary adventure on graph paper. The "players" cast spells and commit imaginary murder, torture, rape, and robbery. A player may stay in the game for days, weeks, or years until he is "killed." Then, through a magical "resurrection," the player can come back to life. "You can kill and maim and bludgeon all you want and never really do it," says one eighteen-year-old player. "It's a great outlet."

Satanic symbols are everywhere. In the Wizard's Workroom, blood (human, dwarven, elven, dragon,) and dung (human, canine, feline, dragon) abound. A container marked "Water," holds holy urine. The old Black Mass of medieval Satanism featured the very same elements.

The fact that D & D includes every aspect of divination forbidden in the Bible should not be lightly dismissed. God instructed the Hebrews before they entered the Promised Land:

When you enter the land which the Lord your God gives you, you shall not learn to imitate the detestable things of those nations. There shall not be found among you anyone who makes his son or his daughter pass through the fire, one who uses divination, one who practices witchcraft, or one who interprets omens, or a sorcerer, or one who casts a spell, or a medium, or a spiritist, or one who calls up the dead.[27]

D & D is not a curriculum staple, but many schools definitely use it. A woman recently phoned us to say her third-grade daughter was given the opportunity to play D & D in her school. A friend from Virginia says this game is offered as an elective in a middle school. We've also heard that D & D is being offered to the talented and gifted in numerous schools.

Why all the fuss? What's so dangerous about Dungeons and Dragons?

A parent in Utah wrote to tell us about the effects of this game on his two sons:

> They stopped doing homework and visiting friends, except to play the game over the phone. Their personalities changed. They constantly argued. . . . It became clear to me that this was more than mythological nonsense. There was a sense of dark and evil foreboding which seemed to affect those who were deeply involved in the game. It was then that I put my foot down and forbade them to play. . . . Soon the game just dropped out of their lives.

If only every D & D experience had that kind of happy ending. But a state trooper from Pennsylvania told us of a fifteen-year-old boy who killed himself during a particularly intense segment of the D & D game. A woman from Florida sobbed to us for forty-five minutes about the suicide of her D & D-playing son. A sixteen-year-old Virginia boy, a gifted student, shot himself in the chest with a pistol the day before his final exams. Sheriff's deputies found his room filled with D & D paraphernalia and a bizarre suicide note that contained mystical phrases believed to be related to the game. We have newspaper articles reporting the suicides of other players. (For more information on Dungeons and Dragons, please see Appendix 2.)

Thankfully, many parents and school personnel are waking up to this problem. A superintendent in Alamogordo, New Mexico prohibited the game after parents complained. But even if the influence of such occult games were completely eliminated, schools still would be dominated by another pervasive force: Humanism.

The Religion of Humanism

Many persons would have us believe that Humanism is simply a form of humanitarianism. They insist Humanists are steering a neutral path between all religions. In truth, however, Humanism *is* a religion with an anti-biblical, anti-God bent. It worships the creature instead of the Creator. If there is any doubt as to Humanism's status as a bona fide religion, the Supreme Court stated in 1961 that:

> Among religions in this country which do not teach what would generally be considered a belief in the existence of God are Buddhism, Taoism, Ethical Culture, Secular Humanism, and others.[28]

Humanists call this reference an "obscure footnote" and claim the allusion to "Secular Humanism" is "an apparent reference to a church in California that calls itself "Secular Humanist."[29]

"Obscure footnote" or not, the Supreme Court has stated that secular humanism *is* a religion. Likewise, a U.S. District Court judge in Virginia declared in 1983 that:

> The First Amendment was never intended to insulate our public institutions from any mention of God, the Bible, or religion. When such insulation occurs, another *religion*, such as secular humanism, is effectively established.[30]

One dictionary defines "religion" as:

> A set of beliefs concerning the cause, nature, and purpose of the universe . . . an organized system of belief in and worship of God or gods . . . something one believes in or follows devotedly.[31]

Based on the examples we've just cited, Humanism, as taught in public school textbooks, clearly fits the definition of a religion.

Abraham Lincoln once asked a critic, "How many legs does a cow have?"

"Four," was the reply.

"If you call her tail a leg, how many does she have?" asked Lincoln.

"Five," was the answer.

"No," Lincoln declared. "Just *calling* a tail a leg does not *make* it a leg."

Calling Humanism a philosophy does not make it non-religious. Humanism sometimes means "humanitarianism" or "humaneness." Occasionally, it refers to classical learning. But in the ideology of "progressive" education, Humanism functions as a religion with defined dogmas. And no religious body ever spoke more dogmatically than this one. Humanists confidently assert that:

(1) Man gradually emerged by chance from lower forms of life over millions of years.
(2) Man creates God out of his own experiences.
(3) Man is his own authority and is not accountable to any higher power.
(4) There are no absolute rules by which to live.
(5) All men should be exposed to diverse "realistic" viewpoints, including profanity, immorality, and perversions as acceptable modes of self-expression.
(6) All forms of sexual expression are acceptable.
(7) Government ownership or control of the economy should replace private ownership of property and the free market economy.
(8) "Global citizenship" should replace national self-determination.
(9) There is no hope of existence beyond the grave—no heaven or hell.[32]

Countless selections and illustrations from textbooks communicate these principles. For example, consider the second dogma—that man creates God out of his own experiences. Current texts are claiming:

God, then, would be the love we encounter when we turn to help others. Prayer would be essentially a dialogue of love. Salvation would be being loved in a community characterized by love.[33]

A NEW GOD. Among all the hundreds of Middle Eastern gods, a very different kind of god emerged. This god was the God of the Hebrews. Here is a Hebrew children's story that tries to explain how people began believing in this new kind of God.[34]

Anthropologists studying human customs, religious practices, ritualism, and the priestcraft came to the conclusion that men created their own gods . . . the gods that men created answered their special needs. The God of the Judeo-Christian tradition was a god created by a desert folk . . . and heaven was high above the desert, cool and pleasant. The Eskimos . . . reversed the concept. . . . To the anthropologists religions were functional; they served men's needs, and they were clearly man-created.[35]

Humanists are aggressive and evangelistic. They are adept at tearing down traditional faith, even if it means permitting the occult to enter the classroom. They are skillful at pouring their anti-God dogmas into the void.

If you don't think Humanists are serious about their efforts, mull over these sentences from *The Humanist* magazine:

The battle for humankind's future must be waged and won in the public school classroom by teachers who correctly perceive their role as the proselytizers of a new faith: a religion of humanity that recognizes and respects the spark of what theologians call divinity in every human being. These teachers must embody the same selfless dedication as the most rabid fundamentalist preachers, for they will be ministers of another sort, utilizing a classroom instead of a pulpit to convey humanist values in whatever subject they teach, regardless of the educational level— preschool, day care, or large state university. The classroom must and will become an arena of conflict between the old and the new—the rotting corpse of Christianity, together with all its adjacent evils and misery, and the new faith of humanism, resplendent in its promise of a world in which the never-realized Christian ideal of "love thy neighbor" will finally be achieved.[36]

Religion is back in the classroom in the form of Humanism, a religion of supreme idolatry that puts man, not God, at the center of all. It is a sad irony that the majority of parents, according to every major poll, still subscribe to the faith of the Bible.[37] But after studying Humanist textbooks, will their children do so?

Footnotes
[1]"Why not pick books from top of the list?" *USA Today*, October 4, 1982, p. 10A.
[2]"Equal Time" answer given to editorials on WCHS-TV, Chan-

nel 8, Charleston, supporting textbooks proposed for adoption, 1974, as reported in James C. Hefley, *Textbooks on Trial*, Victor Books, 1976, pp. 159, 161.

[3]*Church of the Holy Trinity v. U.S.*, 143 U.S. 157 (1892) as cited in James C. Hefley, *America: One Nation under God*, Victor Books, pp. 10-11.

[4]*Ibid.*, p. 11.

[5]*Zorach v. Clauson*, 343 U.S. 306 (1952) cited by Carl Horn, "How Freedom of Thought Is Smothered in America," *Christianity Today*, April 6, 1984, p. 127.

[6]Hefley, *One Nation under God*, p. 11.

[7]*Ibid.*, p. 13.

[8]*Ibid.*, p. 15.

[9]*The Promise of America*, Science Research Associates, Inc., 1970, pp. 40-48.

[10]Hefley, *One Nation under God, p. 20.*

[11]*Search for Freedom: America and Its People*, The Macmillan Company (Benziger), 1973.

[12]The Macmillan Company's September 6, 1972 Reply to Gabler August 8, 1972 Bill of Particulars on *Search for Freedom: America and Its People*, 1973.

[13]*Introduction to the Behavioral Sciences: An Inquiry Approach*, Holt, Rinehart, and Winston, Inc., 1969, p. 170.

[14]*Behind the Mask: Our Psychological World*, Prentice-Hall, Inc., 1973, p. 61.

[15]*School Review*, August 1978, pp. 642-643.

[16]*Ibid.*, p. 643.

[17]*A World History, A Cultural Approach*, Ginn and Co., 1969, p. 31.

[18]Exhibit #5, Texas State Textbook Committee Hearings, 1970.

[19]*The Rise of the West*, Scholastic Book Services, 1976, p. 86

[20]Exodus 14:21-22, NASB.

[21]*Psychology for You*, Oxford Book Company, 1973, p. 191.

[22]*Ibid.*, p. 188.

[23]*Communicating, The Heath English Series*, Grade 3, D.C. Heath and Company, 1973, pp. 142-143.

[24]*People of the World, Teacher Tactics*, Scott Foresman Spectra Program, Scott, Foresman and Company, 1975, p. 50.

[25]*To Turn a Stone*, Skills Handbook, Ginn and Company, 1971, p. 149.

[26]*Ibid.*, p. 150.

[27]Deuteronomy 18:9-11, NASB.

[28]*Torcaso v. Watkins*, 367 US 488 [1961], Footnote 11, p. 495. See also *Washington Ethical Society v. District of Columbia*, 101 U.S. Appellate D.C. 371, 249 F. 2d 127 [1957].
[29]*The Witch-Hunt against Secular Humanism*. A discussion paper by People for the American Way, Washington, D.C.
[30]*Crockett v. Sorenson*. Ruling by Judge Jackson L. Kiser. Bristol, Virginia, 1983.
[31]*The Random House Dictionary*, Random House, 1980.
[32]Precis of *Humanist Manifestos I and II*, Prometheus Books, 1973.
[33]*Relationships: A Study in Human Behavior*, Ginn and Company, 1984, p. 102.
[34]*People and Culture*, The Economy Company, 1982, p. 70.
[35]*Perspectives in United States History*, Field Educational Publications, Inc., 1972, p. 541.
[36]*The Humanist* magazine, January/February, 1983, p. 26.
[37]Substantiated by polls conducted by Gallup, *Better Homes and Gardens*, and Connecticut Mutual Life Insurance Co. See Introduction, footnote five.

AMERICA IS NO LONGER BEAUTIFUL IN OUR TEXTBOOKS

If you were to return to school today, the types of "facts" you'd be taught would simply amaze you. Want an example? Why don't you test your knowledge of history and geography with this little quiz:

(1) Was Benedict Arnold a hero or a traitor? One textbook portrays him only as a hero.[1]

(2) Which men in a fifth-grade history textbook were equated with Jesus dying on the cross? Answer: John Brown, Martin Luther King, and Mohandas Gandhi.[2]

(3) Who deserves more attention in an American history text: George Washington or Marilyn Monroe? One fifth-grade text devoted seven pages to Miss Monroe, while mentioning George Washington only eight times. It said nothing about Martha Washington.[3]

(4) Name the nation you think is being discussed in this passage from another fifth-grade text:

> No nation on earth is guilty of practices more shocking and bloody than is _____ at this very hour. Go where you may and search where you will. Roam through all the kingdoms of the Old World. Travel through South America. Search out every wrong. When you have found the last, compare your facts with the everyday practices of this nation. Then you will agree with me that, for revolting barbarity and shameless hypocrisy, _____ has no rival.[4]

47

Give up? The country so honored is the United States.

(5) Name six major culture areas of the world. If you included the United States and Western Europe in your list, you're wrong—at least according to a world history text which selects:

- The Soviet Union
- Latin America
- China
- India
- Africa
- The Middle East[5]

(6) Is it worthwhile to lose freedom to obtain economic gains? The answer is yes, according to a world geography text which states: "Many people feel that China's economic progress is worth their sacrifice of individual freedom."[6]

(7) True or False. All European countries have representative governments. According to the same world geography book, the answer to this question is, true: "All European countries have some form of representative democracy."[7] The text lists eight such nations—including the Soviet Union.

(8) Fill in the blank. "[In China] _____ turns the people toward a future of unlimited promise, an escalator to the stars."[8] The missing word is, Marxism.

(9) Patrick Henry sounded the watchword of American independence: "Give me liberty or give me death!" Is this line worth memorizing by children? According to a study made by *This Week* magazine, only two of forty-five history texts include that statement.[9]

The Rewriting of History

Hasn't history changed a bit since you were in school? Maybe now you can understand why former-Texas Board of Education member H. Reg McDaniel, M.D., took passages from one such book—which praised Communism while chastising the United States for exploiting children, women, minorities, and immigrants—and concluded they "would do well in pamphlet form to pass out at the Russian Embassy Information Centers around the globe."[10] And why former-Alabama Governor Fob James called another book, that lauded the Soviet Union for "tremendous accomplishments," a "damnable distortion."[11]

Parents also are catching on fast that history hasn't changed—publishers have changed history! A resident of historic Lexington, Massachusetts—the birthplace of the American Revolution—wrote to tell us that:

I have been going to our town PTA meetings and am increasingly worried about the kinds of history textbooks that are being bought for our school system. In my opinion they're not telling the story the way it should be told. . . . The publishers of textbooks are not responding to the needs of American education but only to . . . the propaganda of these liberal educationists.

A poet from Oregon told us:

My husband and I have been screaming about these [distortions of history] for the past thirty years. . . . One of our friends who teaches fifth grade took a whole shipment of books to the dump. She refused to teach her children from a book that extolled the virtues of Communism in general and Fidel Castro in particular. The ACLU attorneys were brought in . . . and the teacher was placed in another school. At any rate, the children lost out in the shuffle. I do feel that children are able to differentiate between bad and good material, and I realize they are exposed to garbage all through their lives, but we don't have to present it in the classrooms with our blessings.

A veteran schoolteacher published this testimony in the *Austin American-Statesman* after the Texas hearings on adopting new government books.

A member of my former school board asked me to review a government book. I labored long and hard and became disillusioned at what I found. Among many questionable points, the publishers made errors of fact; they presented a one-sided version of the subject covered; they advocated one-world government; they condemned nationalism. A child studying such a textbook is not learning facts on which to base his decision; he is being brainwashed.[12]

The educational establishment admits that the "new" histories are based on the personal opinions of the writers. The author of the book which played up Marilyn Monroe and put down George Washington, wrote in the National Education Association journal:

Whatever textbooks are, they certainly are not objective. Isn't it high time, therefore, that all parties frankly admit that what constitutes an "acceptable" textbook depends largely on personal opinion and interpretation? And further that the right to decide which texts are used—and hence to indoctrinate children and prevent them from getting different ideas—rests ultimately with the political faction in power, on its opinions and values?[13]

Politics are indeed involved. But whose political influence dominates? When they don't get their way, educators flay our school boards for voting against their books. We've also found that board members seldom read the books proposed for adoption by the educators' textbook committees, at least not in any detail. They may vote against a book for political reasons, after local citizens object. But the routine political pressures come from the educational establishment upon the school boards. School board members come and go, but liberal educators remain in power indefinitely. History has been changed by publishers, true, but they are merely supplying what liberal educators demand.

Why the Change?

American history didn't come up smelling like week-old limburger cheese overnight. The downplaying of patriotism and putting down of American heroes and principles resulted from a plan by educators who envisioned a *different* future for the U.S.A. As far back as 1913, an NEA committee recommended:

> That historical events be selected with *due regard to their significance*, as illustrations or statements of the social force or conditioning that have made or destroyed the great historical civilizations.[14]

The educators' goal, then, was to choose those "social forces" which they wished to illustrate in negative or positive ways.

Professor George S. Counts of Columbia University, who traveled to the Soviet Union in 1929, presented a paper to the Department of Superintendence of the NEA entitled, "Dare the [American] School Build a New Social Order?" Pay close attention to these two paragraphs:

> There is the fallacy that the school should be impartial in its emphasis, that no bias should be given instruction . . . Professor Dewey states in his *Democracy and Education* that the school should provide a purified environment for

the child . . . this means *stacking the cards* in favor of the particular systems of value which we may happen to possess. Our major concern consequently should be, not to keep the school from influencing the child in a positive direction, but rather to make certain that every Progressive School will *use whatever power it may possess in opposing and checking the forces of social conservatism.*[15]

Speeches and writings by Dr. Counts and other American educators who admired the Soviet system aroused a great deal of enthusiasm—so much so that professors from twenty-four American universities sponsored a special summer session at Moscow University in 1935. John Dewey was among the group that attended. The NEA promoted the summer studies in a full-page advertisement in the March 1935 issue of the NEA's official journal. The curriculum included:

- *Principles of the Collective and Socialist Society*
- *Organization of Public Health and Socialized Medicine*
- *Institutional Changes and Social Backgrounds of Soviet Society.*[16]

In the late 1930s, Dr. Ralph West Robey of Columbia University made a content analysis study of social science texts commonly used in several states. To avoid charges that his research might be biased in any way, he asked a Marxist, a liberal, and a conservative scholar to assist him. When the investigation was completed, Benjamin Fine, education editor of the *New York Times*, interviewed Dr. Robey. Fine noted these conclusions of the study:

> *A substantial proportion of the social science textbooks now used in the high schools of this country tend to criticize our form of government* and hold in derision or contempt the system of private enterprise. . . . There is a notable tendency of the books to *play down* what has been accomplished in this country and to *stress the defects* of our democracy.[17]

Jump now to 1976, the year of America's Bicentennial, when the NEA unabashedly announced its plan of education for a new world under the code word "Global 2000." Here are some arresting quotations from NEA proceedings and from interviews with Association officials:

The Association [NEA] reaffirms that people working collectively can influence and redirect the course of our social history.[18]

The National Education Association believes . . . that the costs and operation of public welfare should be assumed by the federal government and be based on standards of human dignity.[19]

Within ten years I think this organization will control the qualifications for entrance into the [teaching] profession and for the privilege of remaining in the profession.[20]

The United Nations is probably the logical vehicle for bringing about world peace.[21]

I do not believe the Communist states are the biggest obstacles [to development of the international economic order and other global institutions].[22]

We believe that *teachers are the major resource through which to effect a world community based on the principles of peace and justice.* . . . We seek to make history rather than to recall it.[23]

It is with this sobering awareness that we set about to change the course of American education for the twenty-first century by embracing the ideals of global community, the equality and interdependence of all peoples and nations, and education as a tool to bring about world peace.[24]

Who do the educational elite say is the principal enemy of peace and justice? The United States, according to the textbooks and other writings of the ideologues of humanism. In an editorial, associate editor William Murchison of *The Dallas Morning News,* put it better than we could:

The NEA even has a foreign policy—to the effect that the United States must be restrained from blowing up the world. . . . Against the Soviet Union and its daunting nuclear arsenal the NEA has nothing to say. As a Communist *Daily World* reporter wrote of NEA's 1981 convention: "Nowhere in the basic documents of NEA, in their resolutions or new business items, are there any anti-Soviet or anti-socialist positions."[25]

The educational establishment has been drifting leftward for decades. They emphasize liberal concepts in textbooks, and censor out material which would make students proud of our American heritage. The Organization of American Historians, with 12,000 members, surveyed history courses taught in all fifty states and the District of Columbia. Their conclusion: "A movement away from history, at least as history is traditionally defined and taught" is occurring.[26] This is hardly surprising. As the editor of the leading Humanist magazine, *Free Inquiry*, admitted bluntly and honestly:

> The National Council of Churches and the World Council of Churches [along with] . . . many humanist organizations . . . condemn the shortcomings of capitalist countries and reject their foreign policies, but often overlook or excuse all but the most egregious violations of human rights in Communist or third world countries. A similar myopic outlook is held by some members of university faculties who are so enamored with left-wing thinking that anti-Communism is still not considered to be intellectually respectable, whereas anticapitalism is freely accepted.[27]

Picking and Choosing

What scholars of various persuasions say about the leftist anti-American perversion of history is disturbing. But what the textbooks themselves say provides a greater wallop. For much of the rest of this chapter we will quote from textbooks currently being used in public schools. We will mention titles and publishers only in the footnotes so you can concentrate on the content.

One eighth-grade history text censors out Ethan Allen, Nathan Hale, John Paul Jones, David Farragut, and George Washington Carver. Yet it makes note of Bob Dylan, Janis Joplin, Gertrude Ederle, Bobby Jones, Joan Baez, W.E.B. Du-Bois, and many others dear to liberal hearts.[28]

Another text dismisses Patrick Henry as a "prominent leader" of the Revolution without quoting his memorable call, "Give me liberty or give me death." Benedict Arnold's treason goes unmentioned. Francis Scott Key, who wrote "The Star Spangled Banner," is censored. Paul Revere of the famous "Midnight Ride" is simply one of two men who "alerted the Minutemen." But Eugene V. Debs, the Socialist politician and labor leader, is awarded eight pages of accolades.[29]

Of all the genuine American heroes, George Washington appears to receive the most cavalier treatment. The book cited above manages to say of Washington:

> It was only with the utmost difficulty that Washington held a starving army together at Valley Forge, outside Philadelphia, during the winter of 1777-1778.[30]

Compare this with what an older textbook says of the future first President at Valley Forge:

> During this winter, Washington was quartered at the house of Isaac Potts. One day, while Potts was on his way up the creek nearby, he heard a voice of prayer. Softly following its direction, he soon discovered the General upon his knees, his cheeks wet with tears. Narrating the incident to his wife, he added with much emotion, "If there is anyone to whom the Lord will listen, it is George Washington, and under such a commander, our independence is certain."[31]

The fifth-grade history book that gave seven pages to Marilyn Monroe, while mentioning Washington only eight times (and then without telling about his accomplishments) included these interesting comments about Miss Monroe:

> As Norma Jean [her original name] grew older, the boys noticed how pretty she was. When she walked down the street, men turned to watch her. . . . She was pretty. She seemed to know just how to stand and pose.[32]

Ponder the type of discussion questions about Miss Monroe presented to fifth-graders.

> What problems did Marilyn have in her marriage to Arthur Miller? What did she seem to enjoy most about being his wife?[33]

This arbitrary selectivity continues in more recent texts. A 1977 history book gives one line to Pearl Harbor but devotes several pages to the "imperialistic" Spanish-American war. U.S. involvement in all of World War II is allotted only five pages, while a number of chapters extoll the social, cultural, and economic impact of the New Deal.[34]

Methodological Messes

Some books distort history by methodology. One follows a plan of pairing chapters and studying a period of history in light of a notable event. For example, a whole chapter on the Salem witch trials is followed by a chapter on Puritan New England. The students examine the entire Puritan period in the light of witchcraft:[35]

> Two or three hours' discussion of the witchcraft episode, in which questions turn gradually into hypotheses and hypotheses are gradually formalized, sets the stage for reading the following chapter, on Puritan New England.[36]

The teacher is told that "Every generalization in the chapter on Puritanism has to jibe somehow with the events at Salem Village."[37] This information may be all that many students ever learn about our Puritan heritage.

Look at some other pairings in this same book. The early years of the American Republic are examined from the perspective of the actions of conspirator Aaron Burr. The time of religion and reform before the Civil War is measured by the Millerite movement, which erroneously set dates about Christ's second coming. The settlement of the Western Frontier is weighed against the massacre at Wounded Knee. The era of "affluence and anti-Communism" following World War II is considered against the arrest and trial of Soviet spy Alger Hiss. America in the 1970s is epitomized by Watergate.[38]

This book is not a comprehensive and balanced study of history. It is subtle anti-American propaganda. Social problems get top billing while U.S. accomplishments and advantages go virtually unnoticed.

In numerous history texts poverty, protests, and crime are covered far out of proportion to the positive happenings and advances in America. Problems are stressed while solutions achieved through the American system are largely censored. Society and capitalism are blamed for practically everything negative. Ponder this quote:

> But a major reason [for poverty] lies with our society's tragic legacy of prejudice, ignorance, and exploitation, which has left the great majority of adults on welfare poorly equipped for employment by training, education, and even general health.[39]

This, when free enterprise and open opportunity have rendered the lower classes and minorities more upwardly mobile in America than anywhere else on earth.

Work, by the way, is out of favor in many books. We found that one eighth-grade civics text included a welfare application.[40] Why, Norma asked at a textbook hearing, was this included instead of a job application? The publisher belligerently replied that the students were not old enough to work. Norma had done her homework at the local welfare office, so she responded, "Young people can get a job long before they're old enough to qualify for welfare."

Factual Errors

Texts contain numerous factual errors and contradictions as well. One text carries a picture "cropped" to convey the false impression that the National Guard kept blacks from entering Central High School during the 1957 Little Rock integration crisis. The caption states: "A National Guardsman tries to *prevent* Elizabeth Eckford from entering an all-white high school" (our emphasis).[41] Another book shows the complete picture with the caption: "President Eisenhower ordered regular troops and the National Guard to *protect* black students as they went to school at Central High School in Little Rock, Arkansas" (our emphasis).[42]

How many factual errors should be permitted in a textbook? We've read a world geography book which has fourteen errors on one map listing per capita Gross National Product. Eight of the errors favor Marxist countries; five of the other six errors are unfavorable to non-Marxist countries.[43]

The publisher of one world history text acknowledged we were correct when we presented a list of factual errors whose page references covered a full typed page.[44]

The new histories *do* present one trend of American government in a positive and glowing light: paternalistic, benevolent, bureaucratic federal agencies.

"Dad, what did the Founders intend to accomplish when they wrote the Constitution?" my son once asked me. I told him they wanted to create a federal government strong enough to unite the people, while leaving them with as much of their God-given freedom as possible. Most of the governing was to be left up to state and local institutions.

"Not according to this book," he said.

He showed me a list of powers granted to the federal government and a list of limitations on the states. The book said nothing about restrictions on the federal government and nothing about the rights or freedoms retained by the states and people.[45]

That was over twenty-three years ago; we've been reading history, economics, and other textbooks closely ever since. They're still promoting Big Brother bureaucracy. The theme of text after text is that the federal government always knows best. Classical, or free enterprise, economics continues to receive the blame for inflation, unemployment, high interest rates, and every other cloud that appears in the economic sky. The Keynesian theory of government intervention is given high marks, even though many economists have discredited it. The New Deal is credited with ending the Depression of the 1930s when, in fact, the industrial buildup preceding World War II actually set the economy booming again.

Distorting Other Nations

The same propaganda appears at the international level. Government subsidies and foreign aid are considered more effective than private enterprise, even though studies show the opposite more often is true (see: P.T. Bauer, *Dissent on Development*, Weidenfeld and Nicolson; or Melvyn Krauss, *Development Without Aid*, McGraw-Hill). The grandiose schemes of socialist third world governments are touted and their failures hardly mentioned; governments allowing extensive freedom for free enterprise, if not given demerits, are ignored.

The most glowing paeans of praise are reserved for Marxist revolutionaries. How's this one for North Vietnamese leader Ho Chi Minh?

Ho Chi Minh was a man of action rather than one who created new ideas. For over fifty years, he fought for the cause he believed just. This fragile little man inspired genuine love among the people he led. He also won the grudging respect of his enemies.[46]

Left unstated are these facts: For decades, Ho was a dedicated Communist. He eliminated other Vietnamese nationalist leaders through murder or by betraying them to the French. Ho's victories resulted in the death and imprisonment of millions. What textbooks leave *unsaid* often is more damaging than what they *do* say.

Did you also realize that if you're under Communist domination, you're really independent? At least that's what one high school world geography text seems to indicate:

> Except for Thailand, long an independent *monarchy*, the countries of Southeast Asia are newly independent.[47]

This text does not advise students that Vietnam, Cambodia, and Laos are captives of Russian or Red Chinese imperialism. Instead, it notes they all practice "Democratic Centralism."[48]

Here's a glowing endorsement of Chinese Marxism in a text your child may be studying:

> Inspired by the example of the Russian revolution and by the ideologies of Marx and Lenin, the founders of Chinese Communism hoped to free their country from foreign domination and economic backwardness. They set about building strong party organizations and labor unions in the cities of China. They also cooperated with the Kuomintang in efforts to defeat the many regional warlords within China.
>
> [Communist Chinese leader] Mao and his followers carried out land and tax reform in the regions they controlled. They met with peasants and listened to their problems. They explained China's difficulties and urged the peasants to support the revolution.[49]

Your tax dollars pay for the textbooks that glorify Marxist revolutionaries and their revolutions. Dare you insist that the truth be told—that your children be informed that Mao and his Communist allies were responsible for the deaths of at least 30 million Chinese?

Cross the Pacific to Central America. Here's a book that lambasts U.S. foreign policy in Latin America as "interventionist" and "imperialistic." It pontificates that "many progressive Latin Americans" believed the U.S. sent troops to the Dominican Republic "to block necessary and long overdue social reform."[50] The book does not mention that other Latin American leaders believed U.S. soldiers saved the Dominican Republic from becoming another springboard for Soviet Marxism in the Caribbean.

Lest you think this book is an isolated example, let us quote from another standard text:

> Fidel Castro was a leader with charisma (see page 466). Most Cubans saw their caudillo [Castro] as the national revolution personified. A practical politician who felt securely in command, Castro frankly admitted his mistakes. He gave the Cubans a sense of pride in the achievements their small island-nation was making without being tied to its powerful neighbor to the north [the U.S.].[51]

This textbook rhapsodizes Castro's fearless nationalism, his heroic populism, his social compassion, his earthy charisma. It does not acknowledge his Marxist sympathies or Soviet connections, nor does it explain that the Castro regime has made Cuba more economically and politically dependent on Russia than it ever was on the U.S. Finally, it fails to mention that Castro, directly contradicting the impression given here, admitted in 1980 that Cuba still suffers grave economic problems he has been unable to solve.

Twenty years ago, we showed some of the new history textbooks extolling Marxism to a former missionary to Cuba. Having just fled that nation after its revolution, she remarked simply, "Oh, your books have already been rewritten—just like the books in Cuba since Castro took over."

On to Nicaragua:

> Among Latin American countries undergoing political change in the late 1970s, Nicaragua's experience was the most dramatic. A revolutionary movement overthrew the dictator, Anastasio Somoza, Jr., whose family had ruled the country since the 1930s. The revolutionaries took over a ravaged country. They had great difficulty even in maintaining the food supply. The new [Sandinista] government was willing, however, to share power with more conservative politicians.[52]

Professor Neal Frey, a former associate professor of History and Social Science at Christian Heritage College—and now a member of our staff—gave this analysis of the text in which the above quote appeared:

> This book fails to trace the material and increasingly evident ideological links of the Sandinistas and Central

American guerrillas to Cuba and the Soviet Union, or to note the Sandinistas' suppression of opposition newspapers and a "postponement" of free elections in Nicaragua.

Another text observes:

The new Nicaraguan government also wanted to have friendly relations with such revolutionary governments of the third world as Cuba and Vietnam.[53]

Professor Frey responds:

The book does not say that Communist Cuba and Vietnam are Soviet puppet states, but implies they are independent, nonaligned "third world" nations. This is grossly deceptive.

America the Ugly?

The America of our forefathers is not beautiful in textbooks anymore. The welfare state, the United Nations, a hoped-for global world order, and Communist revolutionary movements, are. When we object to slanted discussion and supposedly "open-ended" questions about topics in history, government, and economics texts, our opponents scream that we do not want students to be taught to think. They say we do not want kids to learn about the Great Depression, Vietnam, Watergate, unemployment, or poverty. That isn't true and they know it. We welcome discussion—when the students are given adequate information on *both sides*. We want balance. We simply object to one-sided indoctrination to suit the ideology of the educational establishment.

We believe that young people should be taught the virtues of our American system. What parents would start out by telling their young children all the shortcomings of their immediate and extended family? What's wrong with acquainting children in elementary school with the people and ideas that made this nation great? Texas State Board of Education Chairman Joe Kelly Butler said:

Every kid in the eighth grade needs the advantage of the philosophy that made this country great. Is there anything wrong with making sure that things like "Give me liberty or give me death" are included in . . . texts?[54]

The educational establishment says students should be exposed to a marketplace of ideas. Give everything equal treatment, they argue, and let the students choose. But *they* don't give equal treatment to the issues. A high school U.S. government text, for example, lobbies for gun control without presenting alternative arguments:

> *The rights to freedom and security of the person. . . include the virtually meaningless protection against the quartering of troops in private homes and the insignificant guarantee of the right to keep and bear arms.*[55]

> *Right to keep and bear arms . . . The 2nd Amendment . . . does not* guarantee to any person the "right to keep and bear arms" free from any restrictions by government—nor was it ever intended to do so. The amendment has little real significance today except for its political and propaganda weight in the ongoing controversy over gun controls.[56]

We will deal more extensively with this philosophy of "let the students choose" in a later chapter. For now, we would like to close this chapter with a challenge and warning from H. Reg McDaniel, M.D.:

> Important influences in this country are downgrading and undermining the ideas and ideals that made our country the strongest, most productive, and most benevolent and charitable to other nations in the history of mankind. It is said persons become what they see, hear, and read. The fundamental creeds of what has made us a united people are being eliminated from the educational scene.[57]

Footnotes

[1]*American Adventures*, Scholastic Book Services, 1979, p. 85.
[2]*Search for Freedom: America and Its People*, The Macmillan Company, 1973, pp. 228, 234, 401, 440.
[3]*Search for Freedom: America and Its People*, The Macmillan Company, 1973, pp. 7, 348, 384-390, 403, 412.
[4]*Many Peoples, One Nation*, Random House, Inc., 1973, p. 88. Adapted from a speech by Frederick Douglass and presented to students in the present tense.

⁵*A Global History*, Allyn and Bacon, Inc., 1979, Units Four-Nine.

⁶*World Geography*, Teacher's Edition, Follett Publishing Company, 1980, p. 358.

⁷*Ibid.*, p. 318.

⁸*A Global History of Man*, Allyn and Bacon, Inc., 1970, p. 444.

⁹From an address by the editor of *This Week* magazine, Spring 1962.

¹⁰H. Reg McDaniel, M.D., Bill of Particulars to Texas Adoption Process, *The World, Living in Our World Series*, Harcourt, Brace, and Jovanovich, 1980.

¹¹*Unfinished Journey*, Houghton Mifflin, 1980.

¹²Mrs. B.A. Krueger, "Gablers' attention to textbooks defended," *Austin American-Statesman*, November 20, 1982, p. A11.

¹³William Jay Jacobs, "Whose Textbooks Are They, Anyway?" *Education Week*, March 30, 1983, p. 24.

¹⁴*History Teachers Magazine*, May 1913, p. 136, as cited in "A Bill of Grievances," published by the National Society of the Sons of the American Revolution, Washington, D.C., p. 15. Dr. Counts' paper and many others were presented as part of an exhibit to committees of the U.S. Congress, April 19, 1949, as part of the Proceedings for Investigation of Subversive Propaganda Affecting Public Schools in the Several States.

¹⁵"Dare the School Build a New Social Order?" pp. 19, 24; cited in "A Bill of Grievances," published by the National Society of the Sons of the American Revolution, Washington, D.C., p. 17.

¹⁶*Ibid.*, p. 17.

¹⁷*Ibid.*, p. 13.

¹⁸[NEA] *A Guide Prepared for Faculty Representatives of the United Teaching Profession*, reprinted by *The Freemen Digest*, September, 1978, p. 4.

¹⁹*Ibid.*, p. 15.

²⁰Statement of NEA President George Fisher, 1969, recalled by Michael Lloyd Chadwick in 1978 interview with then-NEA President, John Ryor, as cited in *The Freemen Digest*, September, 1978, p. 25.

²¹*Ibid.*, p. 28.

²²1978 interview by Chadwick with Braulio Alonso, former NEA President and 1978 Director of International Affairs, as cited in *The Freemen Digest*, p. 35.

²³NEA Bicentennial Ideabook, as cited in *The Freemen Digest*,

Sept. 1978, p. 65.

[24]A Summary Report of the NEA Bicentennial Program, as cited in *The Freemen Digest*, Sept. 1978, back cover.

[25]William Murchison, "Who Needs the NEA?" *The Dallas Morning News*, February 17, 1983, p. 18A.

[26]Report by Walden Whitman, *New York Times* News Service, published in *Chattanooga Times*, August 11, 1975, p. 1.

[27]Paul Kurtz, "Democracy without Theology," *Free Inquiry*, Spring, 1984, p. 27.

[28]*American Adventures*, Scholastic Book Services, 1979, pp. 359-361, 443, 466, 594-596, 654, 658, 659, 701.

[29]*History of a Free People*, The Macmillan Company, 1961, pp. 48, 81, 99.

[30]*History of a Free People*, Teacher's Annotated Edition, Macmillan Publishing Co., Inc., 1978, p. 69.

[31]*Barnes' A Brief History of the United States*, 1885.

[32]*Search for Freedom: America and Its People*, The Macmillan Company, 1973, pp. 385-386.

[33]*Ibid.*, p. 390.

[34]*Challenge & Change*, Laidlaw Brothers, 1977, Second Edition.

[35]*Freedom and Crisis: An American History*, Random House, 1978, Second Edition, Chapters 5 and 6.

[36]*Instructor's Manual for Freedom and Crisis: An American History*, Random House, 1978, Second Edition, pp. xiii-xiv.

[37]*Ibid.*, p. xiv.

[38]*Freedom and Crisis: An American History*, Chapters 11, 12, 15, 16, 27, 28, 45, 46, 51, 52.

[39]*Challenge and Change*, p. 453.

[40]*Poverty and Welfare*, Houghton Mifflin Company, 1969, pp. 62-63.

[41]*The Promise of Democracy*, Rand McNally & Company, 1978, p. 365.

[42]*The American Adventure*, vol. 2, Allyn & Bacon, 1977, p. C-90.

[43]*Global Geography*, Macmillan Publishing Company, 1981, p. 104.

[44]Allyn & Bacon, Inc.'s August 1983 Reply to Gabler Bill of Particulars on *The Pageant of World History*, 1983.

[45]*Our Nation's Story*, Laidlaw Brothers, 1954, pp. 165, 167.

[46]*The Pageant of World History*, Allyn & Bacon, Inc., 1983, p. 693.

[47]*World Geography*, Teacher's Edition, Follett Publishing Com-

pany, 1980, p. 348.
[48]*Ibid.*, p. 348.
[49]*People and Nations*, Harcourt, Brace, Jovanovich, 1983, p. 648.
[50]*A Global History of Man*, Allyn & Bacon, Inc., 1970, p. 342.
[51]*Unfinished Journey: A World History*, Houghton Mifflin Company, 1983, pp. 720-721.
[52]*People and Nations*, Harcourt, Brace, Jovanovich, 1983, p. 779.
[53]*A World History: The Human Panorama*, Science Research Associates, Inc., 1983, p. 705.
[54]Saralee Tiede, "Text falls short on patriotism, state board says," *Dallas Times Herald*, November 13, 1982, p. B-3.
[55]*Magruder's American Government*, Allyn and Bacon, Inc., 1979, pp. 177-178.
[56]*Ibid.*, p. 159.
[57]H. Reg McDaniel, M.D., elected member, Texas State Board of Education, letter to the editor, published in *The Stephen F. Austin Maroon*, February 4, 1983, p. 5.

MISEDUCATION IN SEX

If you haven't read your child's textbooks lately, you'd find some of the letters we receive hard to believe. Take this one from a mother in Binghamton, New York:

> This book is sexually stimulating and entirely too graphic in its description of sexual intercourse and how to masturbate. It also puts down parents and the moral way of life. You'd think it was bought at an "adult" bookstore.

Hardly. Her ninth-grader brought it home from school.

Ponder what happened to Julia, one of our staff members. One afternoon, Julia's newly married daughter, Joan, was at our house photocopying some material we planned to take to the Texas State Textbook Committee hearings. While Joan was on a short break, Julia noticed that her daughter was copying some explicit sex education material from a health book. Julia was embarrassed for Joan, so she hurried and finished the copying herself. Joan returned just as the work was completed.

When Joan asked her mother what she was doing, Julia quickly replied, "I didn't want you to see the rest of it."

"O Mother," Joan sighed. "I had all of that stuff when I was in Mrs. Brown's class at school."

Julia's face turned pale. "Honey, Mrs. Brown was your fourth-grade teacher."

"Sure," Joan said. "I remember what she told us. She said, 'This is part of your school studies that you don't take home.

You don't talk about it either, because parents wouldn't understand."

A Sexual Smorgasbord

Lest you think the mother from Binghamton and Julia were a little too sensitive, we'll quote some curriculum your ninth- and tenth-graders may now be studying. We can't print all the material we've seen; the publisher of *this* book would be in trouble if we did. But the following excerpts should be adequate to drive home our point:

> Adolescent petting is an important opportunity to learn about sexual response and to gratify sexual and emotional desires without a more serious commitment.[1]

> In many societies, premarital intercourse is expected and serves a useful role in the selection of a spouse. In such societies, there are seldom negative psychological consequences.[2]

> You are ready for genital sex . . . Feel your nakedness against the sheets of your bed . . . Feel another body alongside yours.[3]

Should twelve-year-olds learn about masturbation? We reviewed one book that used the word "masturbation" an incredible forty-three times in two-and-one-half pages of text![4] This book was being submitted for use by sixth-grade students in Indiana.

How about the caption underneath a picture of two young men embracing in a section titled "Family Health" in a student health book:

> Research shows that homosexuals can lead lives that are as full and healthy as those of heterosexuals.[5]

If you think we're pulling statements out of context, just read this quote from the summary of a section on "Human Sexuality" in a ninth-grade health book:

> (1) A person's biological sex results from a combination of genetic and hormonal influences that operate before birth. One's gender identity develops as a result of social and

cultural conditioning that begins at birth.

(2) The so-called sexual revolution is better termed the gender revolution. Today both men and women are more free to do and be whatever feels comfortable for them.

(3) There are many options of sexual behavior: masturbation, petting, cunnilingus, fellatio, and intercourse. Other partner preferences besides heterosexuality include homosexuality and bisexuality.[6]

Get the idea? A veritable smorgasbord of sex is available. Take what you want, kids, and forget those old-fashioned rules you learned from your family and church.

Kids also are entertained with stories that allow them to feel the emotion of a sexually charged situation. Here's a brief example:

> After rubbing my back for a while, he unhooked my bra. Then he began to touch my breasts.[7]

Students are told in these texts to select and clarify their own values. Teachers mustn't moralize—except *against* the belief that *one* set of sexual values is right. "As sex educators, we are not *telling* them what to do—we are teaching them what we know—as facts, not as truths," says an educator in the *Journal of School Health*.[8] Among other things, this type of philosophy means homosexuality is not to be considered a perversion. Indeed, many books are designed to elicit sympathy and support for gays. This is from a teacher's manual:

> You might point out that it is natural for everyone to have occasional homosexual thoughts or dreams. Emphasize also that there is no reason to avoid homosexuals in normal, everyday, casual contact.[9]

Here are some discussion questions and the "answers" provided for the teacher:

> (5) How common is homosexuality? Should citizens be sympathetic or unsympathetic to the problems of homosexuals? Why?[10]
> [Answer:] As many as 2 to 8 percent of the population may be confirmed homosexual. People should be sympathetic since a person's sex life is his own business as long as it does not offend others.[11]

(10) How does society feel about homosexuals? Why?[12]
[Answer:] As evidenced by legislation prohibiting homosexual acts, American society frowns on homosexuals, as
it does on most things it doesn't understand.[13]

Students discuss laws that prohibit certain sexual acts and
expressions. The teacher's manual for a U.S. government text
includes an activity that instructs students to test pornography
against the First Amendment. The teacher divides the class
into four groups. Group A is to follow a strict constructionist
interpretation of the First Amendment. Group B is to interpret
this Amendment according to national standards regarding the
issue [pornography] at hand. Group C is to decide as they believe the community would. Group D is to decide on the basis of
"their own personal standards or values." Each group appoints
two of their members to play the role of Supreme Court
justices.
   A class member then volunteers to test a porn law "he believes may be wrong or unconstitutional." He describes the action which allegedly broke the law. He and his supporters argue
before the Court why his case should be heard. The justices
then discuss and decide whether or not the Court has
jurisdiction.[14]
   Throughout this exercise, students learn that judicial decisions can be made on the basis of community standards, and
that individuals can decide what's right or wrong "on the basis
of their own personal standards or values." Apparently, the
educational establishment wants to move students away from
firm ethical foundations into the stormy sea of change.

Contraception and Abortion
Some sex education texts suggest that students use contracep-
tives. What if a ninth-grade girl has sex—but forgets to use a
birth control device? Post-contraceptive aid is available at your
local "family planning" clinic. Many sex-ed courses recommend
the services of such clinics. In Kitsap County, Washington, for
example, students were— at last report—being referred to the
Family Planning Clinic in Bremerton where a child could receive contraceptive and/or abortion referral without parental
knowledge or consent. Of the 771 abortions performed in Kitsap
County in one year, over half were referred by this clinic to
medical professionals.[15]

68

Abortion is a little troublesome, but is "probably the oldest human birth control method known," according to a book recently recommended for adoption in Texas. It adds:

> There is no form of birth control or legal abortion that is nearly as dangerous to a woman as pregnancy itself. . . . Abortion was accepted, and fairly common, in the United States and Europe until the early nineteenth century. . . . Religious and ethical opposition did not develop until some time later. The situation has changed since World War II now that the danger of abortion to a woman is again less than the risk of a completed pregnancy, and abortion is, once again, legal in many countries.[16]

Abortion is discussed as an aspect of birth control in both biology and health and homemaking books. The latter tend to spare the students the bloody details. The biology texts are more clinical. One notes:

> There are three main methods of abortion. In *vacuum curettage* and *dilation and curettage* ("D and C") the fetus is sucked or scraped out of the uterus, usually under local anesthesia. . . . These methods are used early in pregnancy. After the fifteenth week of pregnancy, *saline injection* can be used. An injection of salt solution kills the fetus, and the uterus subsequently expels the fetus and the placenta.[17]

Students are never told that such unpleasant realities represent the "murder of the unborn." They are not told that unborn babies may writhe in pain under the abortionist's tools, or that some aborted babies emerge alive and are smothered by medical personnel. Abortion is never described in terms acceptable to defenders of the unborn. The "Right to Life" movement usually is censored from sex education texts.

We'd like to see a few facts like these presented in sex-ed books: *Fortune* magazine estimates that the abortion industry grosses (an appropriate word) half a billion dollars a year.[18] Another source reports that aborted dead babies are being sold from $25 a batch up to $5,500 a pound. During one ten-year period, remains of aborted late-term babies brought in $68,000 for one hospital; the money was used to buy a TV set, cookies, and soft drinks for visiting medical professors.

Equally nauseating is the purchase of fetal collagen by cosmetic makers. Collagen is the gelatinous substance found in the fetus' connective tissue, bone, and cartilage. It subsequently is used as an ingredient in twelve leading shampoos and five hand creams sold throughout this country. Unless the label specifies that *animal* collagen is used, the product probably contains human collagen. It is possible that a schoolgirl could be beautifying her skin and hair with matter from her own dead child.[19] But, of course, sex-ed books would never mention that.

The ugly side of abortion is censored out of texts in favor of a celebration of sexuality and sexual expression. The breaking down of moral standards is hailed as an advance:

> The continual increase in knowledge and changing attitudes toward human sexuality promise to enhance the expression of human sexuality even further in the future.[20]

Sex Education Programs

The citations we've given thus far have come only from material found in textbooks. We haven't even touched on how this information is disseminated through sex education classes and programs.

Parents often are deceived by propaganda about sex education. They recall the hygiene classes of their school days when a doctor or nurse came in and talked to the boys and girls separately about sexual matters. Parents labor under the illusion that today's sex education simply explains the biological facts of anatomy and pregnancy to adolescents. If only they knew!

Sex-ed can start in kindergarten, when a teacher is instructed to take boys and girls on a co-ed tour of bathrooms. By the fifth grade, kids may know more about sex than their parents could find in smut books a generation ago.

Textbook publishers realize that some teachers may have difficulty teaching the new sex-ed. So "helpful" instructions are provided:

> Each instructor uses "sex terms" differently. Write down all the terms referring to body parts and elimination and pronounce them in private, a little louder than necessary, or at a volume level suited to the classroom.[21]

Imagine encouraging teachers to bring such language from the outhouse to the schoolhouse! Teachers are instructed to use terms formerly reserved for latrine walls.

The most explicit and intimate aspects of sexual expression—heterosexuality, homosexuality, and masturbation—are discussed in class. Modesty is out. "Liberated" sexuality is in. Imagine the pressures placed on young people to "grow up" and experience what is freely talked about in the classroom. Imagine the smirks and giggles when someone tries to defend chastity. This constitutes a direct attack upon modesty—one of the virtues many parents still try to teach their children.

The mother from Binghamton told us how her son was treated when she objected to a book dealing with explicit sex:

> His teacher was good about walking over to his desk and saying to our six-foot-two football player, "Jim, if your mommy doesn't like what we are studying, why don't you tell her to enroll you in a private school?" He would never say a word to her when she did this, but she really knew how to hit where it hurts.

Who's Responsible for This Stuff?

How could schools have fallen so far? Who are the planners and policymakers behind this nefarious scheme to strip our children of all modesty and indoctrinate them in the new morality of indiscriminate sexual behavior? Who paid for it all?

We'll take these questions in reverse order. First, the federal government (who else?) has been the sexologists' generous grant giver.

The 1979 federal budget alone offered $338 million to improve health services to adolescents and prevent unwanted teenage pregnancy. Joseph Califano, then-Secretary of Health, Education and Welfare, stated that HEW only *encouraged* sex education; it was up to the local community to decide whether to implement it. But Califano admitted that $2 million was spent on a HEW "task force" which assembled recommendations for what the federal government ought to do in the area of sex education. The "task force" concluded that Washington should evaluate current sex-ed programs in the states and encourage "training for leadership in sex education" among health workers, youth groups, and educators.[22]

The federal spigot continues to pour money into "health education," "population education," "family planning," "responsible parenthood," and other sex-ed vehicles. Additional funds come from state and local education budgets, private foundations, and charities, including the United Way.

The policymakers and planners are principally members of the Sex Information and Education Council of the United States (SIECUS), Planned Parenthood, the NEA, and the national PTA. A SIECUS position paper states:

> Free access to full and accurate information on all aspects of sexuality is a basic right of everyone, children as well as adults. SIECUS looks forward to the day when human beings will be released "from the yoke of fear, guilt, and ignorance about sex.["][23]

David Mace, a past president of SIECUS, takes this view of Judeo-Christian morality:

> The simple fact is that through most of our history in Western Christendom we have based our standards of sexual behavior on premises that are now totally unsupportable—on the folklore of the ancient Hebrews and on the musings of medieval monks, concepts that are simply obsolete.[24]

Planned Parenthood's Five Year Plan called for:

> Universal reproductive freedom . . . making . . . contraception, abortion, and sterilization available and fully accessible to all.[25]

To reach this goal, Planned Parenthood envisioned a national campaign for:

> "Modifying attitudes, behavior changes and/or skills" and abolishing "the arbitrary and outmoded restrictions— legal, regulatory, and cultural—which continue to limit the individual's freedom of choice in fertility matters."[26]

The National Education Association worked hand in hand with SIECUS and Planned Parenthood. The year after Planned Parenthood announced its five-year plan, the NEA stated that:

> The public school must assume an increasingly important role in providing this instruction [sex education] and . . . teachers must be qualified to teach in this area. The Association urges that courses in sex education be developed

with care and that classroom teachers who teach the courses be legally protected from irresponsible censorship.[27]

Translation: Local school officials and parents must not have control over what the schools teach their children about sex.

SIECUS, Planned Parenthood, and the NEA obviously needed the cooperation of the PTA national office to put their program across. Consequently, sympathetic articles appeared in the national *PTA Today* magazine. Lester Kirkendall, Board member of SIECUS and former consultant to the U.S. Office of Education on sex education, advised:

> Just sneak it [sex-ed] in as an experimental course and see how people react. Go to the [local] PTA and get support. That's where the power lies. . . . Always move forward. Say that you are going to enrich, expand, and make it better. The opposition can't stop anything that you have already started.[28]

Kirkendall concluded:

> The purpose of sex education is not . . . to control and suppress sex expression, as in the past, but to indicate the immense possibilities for human fulfillment that human sexuality offers.[29]

A Sampling of Sex-Ed Problems
Sex education definitely has had an impact on the United States—most of it negative. Let's consider a few examples.

First, numerous studies and reports show that teenage promiscuity increases as the number of sex education courses taught in public schools increases. Teenage pregnancy also has jumped alarmingly—the very phenomenon educators promised sex-ed would reduce!

> One of every six [U.S. babies] are now born out of wedlock. . . a third of the babies born to white teenagers and 83 percent born to black teens were illegitimate in a recent year . . . among unmarried teens there are . . .three live births for every five abortions.[30]

Professor Jacqueline Kasun at Humboldt University in California reports one of the most damning studies:

In Humboldt County, where we have several "model" programs and government family planning expenditures per person have been much higher than in the nation, adolescent pregnancy has increased ten times as much as in the nation. The reason this increase in pregnancy has not resulted in an increase in births is that Humboldt County has had a greater than 1,000 percent increase in teenage abortions during the past decade. This increase is more than fifteen times as high as the increase for the nation.[31]

Sweden and Denmark preceded the U.S. in sex education. In 1976, 33 percent of all live births in Sweden were out of wedlock, though half of all teenage pregnancies were aborted. Sweden's National Board of Health reports that venereal disease and illegitimacy rose dramatically the year sex-ed became *compulsory*. Commenting on this development, Dr. Malcolm Tottle states:

> Despite all our efforts to educate young people . . . they just don't seem to care. They have blind faith in penicillin and many of them even think "it's tough" to take a risk.[32]

Denmark's story is, tragically, much the same. Keep in mind that the promoters of American sex-ed once pointed to Sweden and Denmark as the way our schools ought to go!

Sex-ed promoters also concede "some risk" in deciding *who* should teach classes in sex education. "You have to admit that there are people teaching in schools who have sexual problems of their own they haven't worked through," confessed Kirkendall.[33] Did he say deviants or perverts? No, just teachers with "sexual problems." An article on sex-ed in *McCalls* was a bit more candid than Kirkendall:

> The problem is that no screening process for emotional fitness, or even good living-room manners, has yet been devised to keep verbal exhibitionists out of sex education programs. And such people are constantly volunteering to teach.[34]

We're not saying all sex-ed teachers have "problems." We do say, with opinion on all sides to back us up, that teaching sex-ed is more likely than math to attract the wrong kind of teachers. Not only are parents often denied the right to know *what* is taught, but they usually have no say about *who* teaches their children about sex.

Another problem with these programs involves the motivations of those who favor no-holds-barred sex education. In other words, why are some people so excited to see this subject taught in public schools? Dr. Rhoda Lorand, a respected New York clinical psychologist, calls the behavior of such parents and sex-ed promoters "interesting clinically," noting:

> Everyone became an instant authority on mental health, diagnosing those who disagreed with them as "very sick" and "sexually hung-up."[35]

Dr. Lorand wonders whether these "ultra-liberated" parents' enthusiastic reception of sex-ed is a reaction to their own "unconscious anxiety and guilt about sexuality."[36]

Fallout

Sex-ed advocates are hard-pressed to answer these objections. Instead, they denounce their opponents as far right political extremists with sexual inhibitions. Peter Scales, in *The Journal of School Health*, declares:

> Most of these groups [who object to sex-ed] hold the following fundamental attitudes in common: (1) jingoistic patriotism that insists America can do no wrong; (2) "muscular Christianity"; (3) paranoia over imagined conspiracies intent on radically changing society; and (4) an extreme fear of sexuality and information about sexuality.[37]

This quote is from an article in the official journal of The American School Health Association. In the article, the author devoted *one sentence* to the possibility that problems might exist in sex-ed programs. He spent the rest of his paper lambasting the affiliations, tactics, and motives of opponents.

The trumpeters for sex-ed will not admit that their programs have been a colossal and tragic failure. Professor Philips Cutright of Indiana University spelled out this failure in a report entitled, "Illegitimacy in the U.S.: Prepared for the U.S. Commission on Population Growth and the American Future":

> Venereal disease is actually found to increase among children exposed to these programs. . . . The reason for these

negative results is that the programs stimulate much higher rates of sexual activity among the children subject to
them. Yet whenever the problems of teenage pregnancy
are discussed, the only solution seems to be more of the
same.[38]

The sexologists in public education also have ignored
warnings from medical and academic authorities. Dr. Lorand,
who has written and studied extensively in the field of childhood sexuality, outlines these programs' potential harms in a
review of one particular sex-ed course:

> The creators of these [sex-ed] programs regard the child
> as a miniature adult and therefore present him with facts,
> concepts, and demands for self-appraisal which are not in
> harmony with the developmental levels of the child and
> therefore disturb normal development.
>
> Latency age children (five to ten) do not scrutinize their
> thoughts and feelings. Their natural inquisitiveness is di-
> rected to the outer world, and the sensible educator has
> always seized upon this fact to instruct the child in funda-
> mentals. The study of anatomy belongs to puberty when
> the child's interests turn to his body because of pubertal
> changes. . . . When a child is prematurely inundated with
> concepts, anxiety is aroused, learning of academic subjects
> is interfered with, self-confidence and self-esteem are
> damaged.
>
> Parents are criticized, their authority undermined, their
> teaching of the Judeo-Christian ethic diluted, if not indeed
> obliterated, by group discussions in combination with the
> teacher's obvious lack of commitment to chastity.
>
> Most revealing and instructive are the *omissions* from this
> very detailed discussion of sexual activity and its possible
> consequences. They are: the great risks of sterility, espe-
> cially to girls, from gonorrhea and from IUD-caused pelvic
> inflammation. No mention is made of the fact that the
> latest VD scourge, genital herpes, is not only painful and
> dangerous, but incurable at the present state of medical
> knowledge. Not only does it make a girl eight times more
> likely to develop cervical cancer, but it may result in her
> giving birth to a baby that is blind, brain-damaged, suffer-
> ing from other central nervous system impairment, or

dead, even ten years in the future when she may be happily married. One finds no reference to those facts nor to the proven connection between early teenage coitus and cancer of the cervix, coitus under age eighteen having been found to be crucial. One looks in vain for a word of warning about other proven facts: the risk of cervical cancer is greatly increased by multiple partners, by frequent coitus, and by coitus with promiscuous males.[39]

Sex-ed boosters deny their programs are at fault. They blame society, TV, parents, and Puritan hang-ups. Without sex-ed, they claim, teen pregnancies and births would be even greater. But we believe the evidence clearly shows that sex-ed plays a major role in *increasing* what it is supposed to *reduce*. Sex education in curriculum gives legitimacy to immorality. It lends itself to the old "progressive" education principle that students must *learn* by *doing*. It suggests everybody is "doing it." It puts down parents and other adults who want the school to help lift moral values. Sex-ed programs are primarily designed to encourage behavioral change. The biological aspect is only "window dressing."

The sexologists and their allies in education would have you believe that only political and religious conservatives are against sex education in public schools. Dr. Benjamin Spock could hardly be included in this camp. But as the sex-ed drive was getting under way he warned:

> To teach contraception would imply to youths that the school people or parents expect them to be casual, if not promiscuous, in sexual relations. The attitude of adults should be, I think, that sexual intimacy is, ideally, a serious and spiritual matter.[40]

Eunice Kennedy Shriver, Senator Edward Kennedy's sister, said:

> For more than twenty-five years I have worked with teenage girls in trouble. And I have discovered that they would rather be given standards than contraceptives. . . . Nowhere do I hear a suggestion that teenage intercourse can be controlled, that teenagers themselves might want to control it. Society itself may be encouraging teenage sex, and then hypocritically condemning its results.[41]

Listen to the opinion of Dr. Bruno Bettelheim, longtime professor of education at the University of Chicago:

> I think [direct sex education] classes are . . . a danger and that they're implicated in the increase in teenage sex and teenage pregnancies. You cannot have sex education without saying that sex is natural and that most people find it pleasurable. Now what are lonely and dejected teenagers to do with their free time? . . . Sex education cannot teach respect for the integrity of one's own body.[42]

We could give you pages and pages of more warnings. Still, sex education marches on, not so much by mandated programs, but by its integration into standard textbooks, especially health and homemaking books. It's even been considered for inclusion in—of all things—driver education courses. Those of us who know what's going on and protest are pilloried as enemies of humanity. We've dared to challenge the high priests of Humanism!

Taking the Offensive

Former-Rep. Bob Stephenson of Colorado, then-Chairman of the Colorado Legislature's Committee on Education, asked local school systems to provide textbooks for review purposes. Many agencies refused his request; educators screamed he was trying to stir up trouble. But the books Stephenson *did* obtain confirmed his suspicions. Among other objections, he noted a sex-ed book which graphically pictured and explained intercourse and other sex acts, and stated, "Sex is neither fearful nor taboo nor reserved for adults."[43] Educators are still blasting Rep. Stephenson for daring to speak up.

Alice Moore, a minister's wife in West Virginia, was appalled when she saw the new sex-ed curriculum proposed for her local schools. When educators refused to stop the program, she ran for the school board and was elected! She later led the 1974 Charleston-Kanawha County textbook protests, which attracted national attention.

Parents in Burlington County, N.J. forced some major revisions in state-mandated "family life" curriculum. The local Board of Education ordered sex education to be taught in sex-segregated, rather than coeducational classes; had Planned Parenthood films scrapped; ruled contraceptive devices could not be passed around classrooms; and canceled an assignment requiring twelfth-grade students to divulge their innermost thoughts on family and sex.

One of the biggest defeats ever for sex educators occurred in New Zealand. Soon after Norma lectured in that country, parents found that a sex-ed curriculum already was stored in warehouses, ready for distribution to schools. Concerned citizens purchased a full page ad in a national newspaper to alert parents to the garbage that was about to be foisted on their children. The ad caused such a furor that public pressure forced the educational establishment to cancel the distribution of this material.[44]

Here and there we find brave souls who dare to raise their voices and risk the wrath of the self-anointed changers of our children's values. And they *have* been successful! We have in our files a copy of a staff memorandum from a Minnesota school district superintendent ordering his staff not to get involved in "teaching, advising, directing, suggesting, or counseling of students" in abortion and birth control. "Parents," he said, "have the prime responsibility for the inculcation of those moral and spiritual values desired for their children."[45]

Not all parents who object to prevalent sex-ed programs oppose sex education, per se. Their concern is that sexuality and sexual expressions be taught in the context of Judeo-Christian values, in good taste, with the right teacher, and in the proper place.

As we've stated throughout this chapter, the evidence and the opinion of a wide range of knowledgeable and respected authorities indicate that the kind of sex-ed now being given to our children is causing far more harm than good.

Dr. Melvin Anchell, a practicing psychiatrist in Los Angeles, said it quite well:

> The sexuality instinct is one of the strongest that we human beings have, and if we have conscience associated with that sexuality, then we cannot express it like amoebas. But the desensitization program is taking away that conscience and making sex a raw instinct.[46]

> The one thing this sort of sex education is supposed to do for us—that is, help our children become more mature adults—it actually destroys. It does it by interfering with the normal instinctual growth of the child. . . . I think it's creating more perverts than were ever created before.[47]

Footnotes

[1]*Life and Health*, Random House, Third Edition, 1980, p. 161, figure 9.4.

[2]*Ibid.*, p. 161.

[3]*Dr. Block's Illustrated Human Sexuality Book for Kids*, For Kids Only Do-It-Yourself Sex/Life Skillsheet, Storyboard #18, Grades K-12, William A. Block, PREP Publications, 1979.

[4]*Finding My Way*, Bennett Publishing Company, 1979, pp. 206-208.

[5]*Life and Health*, Random House, Third Edition, 1980, p. 164, figure 9.6.

[6]*Ibid.*, p. 175.

[7]*Finding My Way*, Bennett Publishing Company, 1979, p. 59.

[8]*Journal of School Health*, April 1981, p. 209 as cited in *Kitsap Educational Information Council* Newsletter, vol. 1, no. 2, Silverdale, WA 98383, Summer 1981, p. 1.

[9]*Masculinity and Femininity*, Instructor's Guide, Houghton Mifflin Company, 1971, p. 12.

[10]*Masculinity and Femininity*, Student's Edition, Houghton Mifflin Company, 1976, p. 90.

[11]*Masculinity and Femininity*, Instructor's Guide, p. 13.

[12]*Masculinity and Femininity*, Student's Edition, p. 91.

[13]*Masculinity and Femininity*, Instructor's Guide, p. 14.

[14]*United States Government: The People Decide*, Science Research Associates, Inc., 1979, p. 405.

[15]*Kitsap Educational Information Council* Newsletter, vol. 1, no. 2, Silverdale, WA 98383, Summer, 1981, p. 2.

[16]*Biology*, Saunders College Publishing, 1982, pp. 578, 579.

[17]*Ibid.*, p. 580.

[18]*Chattanooga News Free Press*, July 8, 1984, p. A-6.

[19]*Ibid.*, p. A-6.

[20]*Life and Health*, Third Edition, Random House, 1980, p. 175.

[21]*Married Life*, Teacher's Discussion Guide, Chas. A. Bennett Co., Inc., 1976, p. 8.

[22]*Education Daily*, January 25, 1978.

[23]*Sex Information and Education Council of the United States*, Position Statement 1974 as cited in LITE (Let's Improve Today's Education) Newsletter, no. 69, May, 1979, p. 563.

[24]*Sexology Magazine*, April 1968, p. 624 as cited in LITE Newsletter no. 69, May 1979, p. 564.

[25]"A Five-Year Plan: 1976-1980 for the Federation," adopted October 22, 1975, Seattle, Washington as cited in "Bringing the

Sexual Revolution Home: Planned Parenthood's 'Five-Year Plan,' *America*, America Press, Inc., February 18, 1978, p. 114.

[26]*Ibid.*, p. 114.

[27]NEA Resolution 75-11, Sex Education, *"Sex Education: Yesterday, Today and Tomorrow,"* John Tebbel, *Today's Education*, Jan.-Feb. 1976 as cited in LITE Newsletter no. 69, May 1979, p. 565.

[28]*Anaheim Bulletin*, Series of Articles, Dec. 18-20, as cited in LITE Newsletter no. 69, May 1979, p. 568.

[29]*Majority and Minority Reports on Sex Education*, Health and Family Life Committee, Nebraska State Board of Education, 1969, Background Material for the Minority Report.

[30]*Time*, November 9, 1981, p. 67.

[31]Letter from Dr. Jacqueline Kasun to California State Assemblyman Art Agnos, April 4, 1981.

[32]Linner, *Sex and Society in Sweden*, Random House, 1967, Appendix K, p. 191 as cited in LITE Newsletter no. 69, May 1979, p. 571.

[33]*Reader's Digest*, June 1968, p. 83 as cited in LITE Newsletter no. 69, May 1979, p. 568.

[34]"Sex Education," *McCall's*, January 1968, p. 116 as cited in LITE Newsletter no. 69, May 1979, p. 568.

[35]"A Psychoanalytic View of the Sex Education Controversy," Rhoda L. Lorand, Ph.D., reprinted from *Journal of New York State School Nurse Teachers Association*, vol. 2, no. 1, Fall 1970, p. 36.

[36] *Ibid.*, p. 36.

[37]*Journal of School Health*, April 1981, p. 300 as cited in *Kitsap Educational Information Council Newsletter*, vol. 1, no. 2, Silverdale, WA, Summer 1981, p. 1.

[38]"Bringing the Sexual Revolution Home: Planned Parenthood's Five Year Plan," *America* Magazine, February 18, 1978.

[39]Correspondence with Mrs. Carolyn Reas, *Cause*, February 17, 1979.

[40]*Redbook*, January 1969, Benjamin Spock, M.D., "Is Contraception a Proper Topic in Sex Education?" as cited in LITE Newsletter no. 69, May 1979, p. 570.

[41]Eunice Kennedy Shriver, "There Is a Moral Dimension," *Reader's Digest*, November 1977, p. 153.

[42]Interview with Dr. Bruno Bettelheim by Elizabeth Hall, "Our Children Are Treated Like Idiots," *Psychology Today*, July

1981, as cited in *Kitsap Educational Information Council* Newsletter, vol. 1, no. 2, Silverdale, Washington, Summer 1981, p. 4.

[43]The book cited by Rep. Stephenson is *Sex, with Love—A Guide for Young People* by Eleanor Hamilton, Ph.D. It is used in Denver area schools.

[44]*The New Zealand Herald*, October 4, 1977, Auckland, New Zealand, sec. 2, p. 7.

[45]South St. Paul Public Schools, Special School District no. 6, Center Bulletin no. 39; 1974-1975 from Ray I. Powell, Superintendent of Schools to All Administrators, February 26, 1975.

[46]*Congressional Record*, February 7, 1969, E969, as cited in LITE Newsletter no. 69, May 1979, p. 567.

[47]*Ibid.*, p. 568.

CHAPTER SIX

LESSONS IN DESPAIR

Jack be nimble
Jack be quick
Snap the blade
And give it a flick
Grab the purse
It's easily done
Then just for kicks
Just for fun
Plunge the knife
And cut and run. . . .[1]

This poem is from a very popular poetry book, written as adult satire. But it also is found in many, many public schools. In fact, one eighth-grade English composition text suggests that students model their own poetry-writing after such poems.[2]

If you think children read only bright, wholesome, happy poems and stories in school, think again. One columnist notes:

> If you are naive enough to believe, as the "father" of public school education Horace Mann wrote around a century ago, that school can rescue 99 of every 100 children "from uncharitableness, falsehood, cupidity, licentiousness, violence and fraud and reared to the permanence of all duties, and the practice of all the kindness and courtesies of domestic social life" . . . you'd better open your eyes or have your head examined.[3]

In many instances, school children are receiving just the op-posite—lessons in violence, despair, hopelessness, and law-breaking. Naturally, we're not implying that teachers tell stu-dents, "It's OK to go out and hold up a grocery store, kill someone, or kill yourself because life isn't worth living." But we *do* believe that kids can get such ideas from textbooks which do not make moral judgments over whether certain behavior is right or wrong.

Let's dip into our mailbag for a few comments on this subject.

Here's a letter from a mother in Moore County, Tennessee:

> We have found the content of [our son's seventh-grade English textbook] to be . . . depressing, morbid, confus-ing, sometimes violent, and containing stories where lying and stealing are passed over and/or where such behavior ends in gains for the ones practicing these things.

A parent from Seabrook, Texas laments:

> "Quality" education in this state almost destroyed my sons. When my oldest was ten and in the fifth grade he would cry every day and plead not to be sent to school. It was just too terrible for him and I couldn't understand why. He said he would rather die and would kill himself first. I just couldn't understand. . . . I went to school, got his book, and began to read. I read the whole book and was depressed.

Another mother who complained about the reading text for her seventh-grader told us:

> She [the teacher] insinuated I was ridiculous and my daughter was hearing horrible language on the bus and in school, etc., and how can I protect her, and on and on. I told her that I felt the school curriculum and teachers should set an example. . . . The teacher never once said she understood how I felt or thought I had a point. She was just plain rude. By the way, she told me they had been reading this book for eight years and I'm the first parent who ever complained.

Many educators respond in this fashion—and often are less than honest in doing so. We've complained *repeatedly* about the lessons textbooks teach with regard to law-breaking, despair, and violence. Parents in Charleston, West Virginia were so enraged over the force-feeding of degrading literature to their children that 8,000 of them marched down the streets of Charleston shouting: "Two, four, six, eight; We don't want your books of hate." No one can say parents aren't complaining about the quality of textbooks.

Hate, Violence, and Despair
Here's an example of what seventh- and eighth-graders must read in some schools:

> "Aw, sock the yellowbelly!" Marty heard Gelberg say, and he smacked the kid as hard as he could on the shoulder. The kid screwed up his face to keep from crying, and tried to back through the fellows ringed around him.
> "Lemme alone!" he yelled.
> Marty looked at him fiercely, with his jaw thrust forward, and felt his heart beating. He smacked the kid again, making him stagger against Arnie in back of him.
> "Yeah, yellowbelly!" Marty hollered, feeling how the fellows were on his side and how scared the new kid was. He began smacking him again and again on the shoulder.
> "Three, six, nine, a bottle of wine, I can fight you any old time!" he yelled. With each word he smacked the kid on the shoulder or arm. At the last word he swung with all his strength. He meant to hit the kid on the shoulder, but at the last instant, even while his arm was swinging, something compelled him to change his aim; his fist caught the kid on the mouth with a hard, wet, socking sound. The shock of his knuckles against the kid's mouth, and that sound of it, made Marty want to hit him again and again. He put his head down and began swinging wildly, hitting the new kid without any aim on the head and shoulders and arms.
> The new kid buried his head in his arms and began to cry. "Lemme alone!" he yelled. He tried to rush through the fellows crowded around him. With all his might Marty smacked him on the side of the head. Rushing up behind him Arnie smacked him too. Paulie Dahler shoved the skullcap, with its paper clip ornaments, over the kid's eyes; and as he went by Gelberg booted him in the pants.
> Crying and clutching his cap, the new kid scampered over to the curb out of reach.[4]

Actually, this one story is mild compared to much of the stuff we've seen in school readers—graphic accounts of gang fights; raids by wild motorcyclists; violent demonstrations against authority; murders of family members; rape.

Consider this narration depicting a girl waiting to kill the brother she hates:

> She picked up a long knife which one of the boys had used to cut bread, and looked at its sharp-scraped edge. She would kill him. She sat straight in her chair, one hand resting on the table, the other holding the knife between her knees, concealing it in the folds of her nightgown. She kept her eyes steadily on the door, and Len came in. He looked at her, startled, and then glanced away. He started to walk around the table. "In a minute," she thought, "he'll pass me, and then his back will be turned. Then I'll kill him." Her fingers tightened on the handle of the knife.[5]

This eighth-grade book also includes a story about a young couple tempted to push a button to kill someone, a TV play about two hitchhikers who are threatened and nearly beaten, and a poem written in the language of a two-year-old.

Just when we thought things couldn't get much worse, we read a story about a group of men who land on another planet called The City. Twenty thousand years earlier, a terrible disease—brought by earthmen—killed The City's inhabitants. Now, as revenge is executed, men are cut open, their bodies emptied, and organs replaced with electronic parts. They are computerized to return to earth and kill its people through the introduction of disease organisms.

We entered the following excerpt from this story into the record of a Texas textbook review hearing:

> Hung by his feet, a razor drawn across his throat, another down his chest, his carcass instantly emptied of its entrails. Exposed upon a table under the street, in a hidden cell, the captain died. Great crystal microscopes stared at the red twines of muscle; bodiless fingers probed the still pulsing heart. The flaps of his sliced skin were pinned to the table while hands shifted parts of his body.[6]

We also entered a portion of a "nice" little poem called "Sea Lullaby" into the Texas record:

The sea creeps to pillage,
She leaps on her prey;
A child of the village
Was murdered today.

She came up to meet him
In a smooth golden cloak,
She choked him and beat him
To death, for a joke.

Her bright locks were tangled,
She shouted for joy,
With one hand she strangled
A strong little boy.[7]

First- and second-graders are not exempted from frightening stories. "The Travels of a Fox," tells the story of a fox planning to eat a little boy. The publisher suggested the story be read five times "for sound educational reasons." This same book includes pictures of a young boy running into an abandoned house where he has to hide in a closet when robbers enter the room.[8]

The fourth-grade edition of this text series shows pictures of young children stealing fruit and hubcaps. Pupils are instructed to:

> Study these pictures. They may help you to make up a realistic story. . . . Or you may want to tell it in the first person, by using *I* for the main character.[9]

In other words, in the first person, a student would be required to say, "*I'm* stealing fruit," and "*I* stole hubcaps."

The teacher's edition for the second-grade book tells the instructor not to moralize. The teacher is to allow "the children," when talking about the stories, to decide right and wrong for themselves.

Oh, yes, some of the stories are sprinkled with profanity. Fortunately, in Texas, the State Board of Education adopted a rule against profanity and obscenity in textbooks after seeing some which were flooded with unwholesome material. But many states do not have such a rule. As a result, material is provided to children which family newspapers would never dare to print.

We counted seventeen obscenities in eighteen lines in a history book, plus four expletives in an article using God's name sacrilegiously.[10] The publisher responded to our protest:

> These oaths seem to be more prayerful than blasphemous. To whom does one appeal if not to God, when all seems lost and the hopelessness or horror of a situation is apparent?[11]

Prayerful cursing? If this were genuine piety, as the publisher pretends, be assured it would have been censored in the name of "separation of church and state."

The Pervasiveness of These Themes

Too much of the literature which children are required to study in public schools follows depressive, negative themes. Under the heading, "negative thinking," we developed these categories for books we review.

(1) Alienation
(2) Death and suicide
(3) Degrading or humiliating
(4) Depressing
(5) Discontentment
(6) Frightening and horrifying
(7) Hate inspiring
(8) Lack of respect
(9) Low goals
(10) Lack of motivation
(11) Problems stressed
(12) Skepticism promoted

In many texts, these themes predominate over the few stories that stress goodness, generosity, honesty, respect for law, love of country, honor of parents, motivation for attaining high goals, and simple beauty.

The negativism and sordidness of American textbook literature has spilled over into other Western nations. Parents from more than twenty-five foreign countries have contacted us about the problem.

While Norma was on a speaking tour of Australia she came across an unusually bad book for middle schools. She only had time to review one chapter called "The Killers" before speaking to a group of parents and teachers.

The chapter began:

KILLERS (and their victims)
Tell a story. YOU are a murderer. WHOM do you mur-

der? WHY? (You may think you are completely justified.)
HOW do you do the terrible deed? Describe it in detail.
How do you feel—as you work out your plans? as the
victim's last moment approaches? at the instant of the
slaying? afterwards? What happened?
TURNABOUT
YOU are the victim of a murderer.[12]

A few pages later, Norma noted, the children were to divide
into groups and discuss what they thought should happen to
each of the following killers: A drunk driver who killed a child
on a bicycle. A man who slipped up behind another and cut his
throat. A strict Buddhist who killed a rat—a gross violation of
his religion. A brave cowboy who shot a dishonest city busi-
nessman in a gunfight. A New Guinea tribesman who killed a
member of another tribe in revenge. A doctor who deliberately
injected an overdose of morphine into an aged patient with
incurable cancer.[13] This exercise ended with the question: "How
old would you have to be before you would be ready to kill
somebody?"[14] Students then were instructed to collect reports
of killings from one day's newspapers and to keep a record of
murders on TV.[15]

Later in the same book, Norma spotted a short story entitled
"Fear." Here's a brief excerpt:

Maris said: It served Rewi Tamati right. He shouldn't
have killed the girl.
Peter said: If they weren't all cowards, they would have
gone and fought him. It wasn't wrong to kill him—it was
the way they did it that was wrong.
Max said: If we'd been living then we'd have done the
same, so you can't say it was wrong.[16]

As Norma spoke, the parents became extremely upset. During the hubbub, a man jumped up and announced that as a
representative of the book's publisher, he should be heard.
The moderator said no, but Norma whispered, "Let him
talk."
The publisher snapped, "Why are you bothered about this
chapter? There are seven more like it."
Somebody yelled, "Isn't it true that the author of the book
you're talking about committed suicide?"
The publisher didn't deny that. Parents and teachers then

began shouting at him and at one another.

"Please, please," the representative finally asked the moderator, "may I sit down?" As he retreated to his seat, he was overheard to say, "I wish I had never stood up."

Death Education

Death education has been slipping into curriculum material under the rationale that schools have a mandate to teach "the whole child." But just consider the content of some sample lessons.

One text asks students, "What would you like to have written on your tombstone? Give your answer in twenty words or less."[17] A sixth-grade social studies text devotes five pages to "The Final Rite of Passage."[18] And a homemaking text suggests to eleven-year-olds that death can be a "pleasant experience."[19]

A health text describes dying as an orgasmic event:

> The thought of death sometimes occurs in a sexual context . . . in that the event of orgasm, like the event of dying, involves a surrender to the involuntary and the unknown.[20]

The humanistic architects of death education never present the Christian hope of life after death. They give the students the depressing pagan doctrine that this life is all there is and death ends everything; or, they merely treat a belief in life after death as an opinion—neither true or false.

Here's an exercise that's presented above a half-page picture of Jacqueline Kennedy and her daughter, Caroline, kneeling before the casket of assassinated President John F. Kennedy:

> There are no right and wrong answers to these questions. Choose the answers that seem best for you.
> (1) Is there life after death?
>   Strongly believe there is
>   Might be
>   Not sure
>   Probably not
>   Sure there is not[21]

Death education is not the business of public school education. It is one more example of how humanism has trespassed into a domain that belongs to family and faith.

Role Playing

Role playing is a much-used tool in education today. This device stirs deep emotions within students and brings self-revelations that often are unwarranted in a classroom setting. Role-playing situations reported to us from Maryland include:

> Role play being drunk and coming home to find your parents sitting in the living room with friends. How would you get past them without their knowing? (Seventh-grade English class)

> Role play your mother finding marijuana in your bedroom. (Eighth-grade English class)

> Role play: "A boy with several years of schooling ahead of him is confronted by a girl he has been dating. She tells him that he is the father of her expected child, and she demands that he marry her. If neither professes to love the other, what should they do?" (Tenth-grade home economics class)[22]

While we have not yet seen an assignment asking students to role play an act of suicide, we *have* seen stories, poems, and articles which make students think of suicide—particularly if they have emotional problems and are depressed. We mentioned a poem entitled "Resume" in our Bill of Particulars to the State of Texas in an attempt to prevent the adoption of a tenth-grade English text:

> Razors pain you;
> Rivers are damp;
> Acids stain you;
> And drugs cause cramp.
> Guns aren't lawful;
> Nooses give;
> Gas smells awful;
> You might as well live.
> A: Yeah, you might as well live.
> B: Suicide *is* a bit grim.
> A: Now, if only I could think of a *better* way. . . . [23]

Why Do Schools Use These Materials?

Why do educators foist such material on captive students? Actually, it's part of a program which has dominated public education for decades. The National Education Association laid it out in 1934:

> The major problem of education in our times arises out of the fact that we live in a period of fundamental social change. In the new democracy, education must share in the responsibility of giving purpose and direction to social change. The major function of the school is the social orientation of the individual. . . . Education must operate according to a well-formulated social policy.[24]

Thus, "pluralism" and "realism" became code words under this plan for directing social change. Social psychologist Otto Klineberg compared fifteen American reading primers, including one called *Fun with Our Family*, and concluded that the characters—"gentle and understanding parents, doting grandparents, generous and cooperative neighbors, even warmhearted strangers"—were too *good*. He recommended that frustration, meanness, poverty, and crime be added for balance. Get this: He advised that educators study books used in the Soviet Union and Sweden to discover the levels of realism small children could handle.[25]

Klineberg wasn't the first or last person to advocate these notions, but his ideas illustrate the crusade to censor from texts the Judeo-Christian virtues of family affection, respect of parents, work, thrift, independence, and achievement.

Here's an example of how this negative philosophy worked its way into a speech book:

> Take a look, Whitey, take a good, long look at your beautiful cities with your elegant suburban homes of green grass. Look at your stately churches with their carpeted aisles and stuffed offering plates. Look at your children who never dream of driving anything but the newest cars . . . who've never known the bitter taste of poverty. Take a look, Whitey, and pray. Pray to your Whitey God Who died before He was born. Pray to the Man Whose dream of equality faded away as you, Whitey, nailed Him to the cross. Take a good long look, Whitey, and pray, because this time it's going to be different. This time you're going to burn, baby, burn![26]

When we object to such incitements to violence and stories of blasphemy, rape, and murder, educators invariably say, "But

the Bible contains such realism. Would you censor out the violence of Samson and David?" This only shows the Humanists'
lack of moral perception. The Bible clearly distinguishes right
from wrong and prescribes punishment for wrongdoing. Current books which contain stories and articles about violence,
crime, and rebellion make no such moral judgments.

Humanist educators claim they are exposing students to good
literature. The educational journal, *Teacher*, praises stories
which feature wife beating, gang beatings, knifings, and
muggings for their "excellent literary quality."[27]

What's our response to this deplorable situation? Columnist
Barbara Morris takes the words right out of our mouths:

> Why can't books be offered that are "well written" and "of
> excellent literary quality" that portray beauty, compas-
> sion, friendship, devotion, hope, trust, joy, loyalty, hones-
> ty, and courage—books that elevate the human condition
> and stimulate the goodness of human beings? Why dwell
> on the worst that humans can be? Is it because these
> positive emotions and virtues do not offer enough opportu-
> nity to clarify a child's values or to invade his personal or
> family privacy in order to do some social engineering?[28]

Would that these books did lift up goodness! Unfortunately,
we have a whole generation of educators who have been indoctrinated to believe that children need to be shocked and shaken
instead of being taught the moral and cultural principles on
which America was founded.

We Are What We're Taught

Norma once spoke to parents and teachers near Sydney, Australia about the negativism and violence found in textbooks.
Several young teachers mocked, insulted, and ridiculed her for
daring to question the new trends in education. Finally, the
principal of a Catholic school, a tall, elegant nun, stood up and
stated:

> I can't stand this any longer! You're acting like a bunch of
> children. What Mrs. Gabler says is true and you ought to
> know it. Always in the past, we saw the need to teach the
> good, the true, and the beautiful. Now we teach fear,
> violence, and frustration, and our society is becoming ex-
> actly what we're teaching.

Publishers and educators cannot deny the shocking increases in suicide, murder, thievery, vandalism, drunkenness, drug use, and promiscuity among young people in recent years. Between 1950 and 1980, suicides in the fifteen-to-twenty-four-year-old age-group increased almost 300 percent, while the suicide rate for the total population grew by 11 percent.

Sociologist Ronald Maris blames family pressures, drug and alcohol abuse, promiscuity, lack of self-esteem, and a sense of hopelessness, for this horrifying trend.[29] Public school textbooks, we believe, are a central part of this dismal picture. The negativism they present serves only to aggravate family tensions and reinforce the sense of hopelessness many students feel. Combined with the emphasis textbooks place on "situation ethics" and "individual autonomy," how can students be expected to develop constructive values?

Violence "of excellent literary quality" has washed back into the schools. Willard McGuire, a recent president of the NEA, notes that students physically attacked more than 110,000 teachers—one in twenty—during the course of one school year. Many teachers, he says, do not report violent incidents because they do not wish to tarnish their school's reputation.

Pranks always have been part of the school scene. But today, Mr. McGuire notes with sadness, teachers are faced with assaults, murders, robberies, extortion, and rampant vandalism. One example: A bright fourteen-year-old student came to school in Austin, Texas and shot one of his teachers to death in the presence of horrified classmates.

Educators and textbook publishers hide behind their robes of self-righteousness and blame the family, society, and low teacher salaries for the upsurge of violence and lawlessness among young people. We have never heard one member of the educational elite admit that the social orientation of curriculum is a part of this problem.

Speaking Out

We've battled negativism and violence in textbooks since the 1970s. Our Bill of Particulars concerning a series of federally funded English texts for high school noted that:

> These books . . . contribute to rebellion, lack of respect for authority, sadism, violence, and disillusionment . . . they will most certainly defeat the whole purpose for

studying literature in our schools. . . . If these books are the only literature presented for a whole school term to high school students, then it becomes understandable why youth wishes to escape through drugs, suicide, or any other possible means. It is also evident that the course is designed to form definite attitudes in the student, rather than enrich his life through reading fine classics.[30]

At a 1975 textbook hearing, Fran Robertson and another mother dramatized their objections to violence contained in several school books by placing red tabs at the numerous references to death, suicide, and killing made in these texts.[31] They held up the red-tabbed books and pleaded they not be taken. Their pleas were ignored; the books were approved.

Despite such setbacks, we kept complaining and objecting. Parents' groups across the country screamed. Finally, the cry against negativism and violence in literature texts became so great that the elected Texas Board of Education put publishers on notice: Texas would no longer accept books filled with negativism and violence. The publishers got the message. Two years later the textbooks offered to our state were greatly improved. But from the letters we receive, books loaded with violence, negativism, and despair still are being widely used in school districts across the country.

Our "druthers" would be to bring back real character education, as was taught in the *McGuffey Readers*, the most popular curriculum series ever published—stories with positive points, stories that exalt honesty, virtue, decency, family, and sexual morality. All we want is good literature with a wholesome purpose.

You may think our efforts simply reflect syrupy, moralistic, middle-class values. Call them whatever you like. But we guarantee that the use of better textbooks would improve our schools and increase the likelihood of our children emerging as good citizens and worthy leaders of the next generation.

Footnotes
[1]*The Inner City Mother Goose*, Simon and Schuster, 1969, p. 26.
[2]*Language 8*, The Laidlaw Language Program, Teacher's Edition, Laidlaw Brothers, Publishers, 1983, p. 147.
[3]Ellen Goodman, "Bell Rings for Future," *Dallas Times Her-*

ald, September 8, 1982.

4*Projection in Literature*, Scott, Foresman and Company, 1976, pp. 225-226.

5*A Place To Be*, The Voices of Man Literature Series, Addison-Wesley Publishing Company, 1970, p. 76.

6*New Voices in Literature, Language, and Composition 4*, Ginn and Company, 1978, p. 221.

7*Ibid.*, p. 267.

8*Communicating, The Heath English Series*, Grade 2, D.C. Heath and Company, pp. 15, 89.

9*Communicating, The Heath English Series*, Grade 4, D.C. Heath and Company, 1973, p. 113.

10*Liberty and Union: A History of the United States*, Teacher's Edition, Houghton Mifflin Company, 1973, p. 425.

11Houghton Mifflin Company's September 8, 1972 Reply to Gabler Bill of Particulars, Texas State Textbook Adoption Process, 1972.

12*Messageways on a Small Planet*, Cassell Australia Limited, 1974, p. 135.

13*Ibid.*, p. 138.

14*Ibid.*, p. 138.

15*Ibid.*, p. 139.

16*Ibid.*, pp. 140-141.

17*Let's Talk about Health*, Cebco Standard Publishing, 1980, p. 31.

18*Around Our World*, Houghton Mifflin Company, 1980, p. 151.

19*Homemaking Skills for Everyday Living*, Goodheart, 1981, p. 152.

20*Life and Health*, Random House, 1976, p. 486.

21*Let's Talk About Health*, Cebco Standard Publishing, 1980, p. 31.

22"The Impact of Federal Involvement on Public Education," Maryland Federation of Republican Women Study Guide, 1976, pp. 6-7.

23*New Voices in Literature, Language, and Composition 2*, Ginn and Company, 1978, p. 359.

24Willard E. Givens, "IV. *Education for the New America*," 1934 Annual Proceedings of the NEA, Department of Superintendence, pp. 653-654. Dr. Givens subsequently became executive director of the NEA.

25Cited in *Chronicles of Culture*, September/October 1981, "Comment" by Allan Carlson, p. 4.

[26]*Speech-Communication: A Modern Approach*, Addison-Wesley Publishing Company, Inc., 1973, p. 211.

[27]Rose Blue, "Violence in Children's Literature: Can You Make Positive Use of It?" *Teacher*, January 1979, p. 63.

[28]Barbara M. Morris, "The Real Issues in Education as Seen by a Journalist on the Far Right," *Phi Delta Kappan*, May 1980, p. 614.

[29]*U.S. News & World Report*, April 2, 1984, p. 48.

[30]Exhibit 18, Texas Education Agency, Compilation of Bills of Particulars, pp. 118, 121, *Macmillan Gateway English* Series, Macmillan, 1970.

[31]*Signposts*, Scott Foresman Reading Systems, Grade 7, and *Milestones*, Scott Foresman Reading Systems, Grade 8, Scott, Foresman and Company, 1975.

CHAPTER SEVEN

CHILDREN ADRIFT

Here is a parable of what is happening to our children in humanistic education today.

Imagine that fifty young children are picked up from their homes and bused to a marina. Each will board his or her individual boat, and be put to sea equipped with all the necessary provisions—except a compass and map.

The children arrive at the dock. They babble excitedly as instructors direct them to their boats and show them how to operate the motor and other equipment. "Only one to a boat," the chief instructor says. "You may steer your boat as you wish. A group of you may want to travel in a fleet, or you can motor alone if you wish. Just follow your feelings."

Some of the children's parents have warned them to watch out for dangerous reefs, treacherous straits, and islands populated by cannibals. "That's good," the chief instructor says, "but remember you're independent of your parents and on your own now. You make the decisions. The sea has changed since your parents made their voyages. You select the direction that seems best for you."

So the children are launched in their frail little boats while their parents stay home with mixed feelings. Most parents—remembering the wise guidance they had when setting out on their voyage of life—trust the schools implicitly. But some have heard disquieting reports: the schools have changed; children are being poorly equipped for this voyage. Students are being sent on their own without maps or a compass. But these troubled parents cannot afford to moor their children in safer ports. So they must, by law, send their children to this marina and trust that all will be well.

The children are launched. The instructors fly overhead in helicopters, gauging their progress. Look, there's little Johhny, headed toward an underwater reef. His boat will smash! He could be drowned! But don't worry, an instructor sees him and surely will wave him back. Wait! Has the instructor gone mad? He is telling Johnny, "Keep going in the direction you feel is right!"

There is Jane, the dimpled little apple of her daddy's eye. Jane is traveling with a group toward an island of cannibals. Surely her instructor will warn her and her friends. No, he simply circles overhead, shouting, "Go with what the group thinks is right."

Absurd? Ridiculous? Improbable? It happens every day! This parable parallels exactly what is occurring in our humanistic schools. Young children are being taught there are no moral absolutes, no fixed rules of life; they're being dispatched into the world to find their own way. This fact confronts us in every report we hear on juvenile behavior. Rising sexual promiscuity, vandalism, drug abuse, thefts, assaults, drunken driving, and suicides all point to problems in the schools.

The Parable Applied

For over two decades we have called attention to how text-books are attacking the moral principles which still hold families and the nation together. Yet the educational establishment stubbornly insists on making every child his own skipper amidst the dangerous currents of life.

We've been ridiculed and castigated, flayed and derided by educrats and their minions who claim our children belong to the school, that they alone know how to teach young people. These "change agents" hold a much more permissive value system than the great majority of parents.[1] Yet they claim that we, who have no vote on any textbook committee or school board, are intolerant censors. They seldom even answer our objections specifically. They just keep screaming the same old dirty charges, hoping that people will not pay attention to us, hoping that we'll simply go away. Neither is about to happen.

Please understand. We are not against intellectual inquiry. We simply do not want to put young minds ashore on "strange islands devoid of recognizable landmarks and guideposts."[2] We strongly believe that schools should come out firmly in favor of the morals and principles which the great majority of Americans hold.[3] Some teachers do, and risk official rebuke or court action for their courage. But most textbooks continue to present only amoral humanistic ideology. One text, for example, asks students the following question (the "correct" answer, from the teacher's manual, is in parentheses):

> From whom might you resent getting some *unasked-for* advice about how to dress, how to wear makeup, or how to behave? Why? (From some teachers, from "old-fashioned" parents, from bossy older brothers and sisters, etc.)[4]

Value-Free Education

Humanistic educators insist that they do teach values. But they also insist that values must be taught in a "value-free" way to avoid teaching religion. This is a humanistic cop-out. Humanism teaches the religion of moral relativism, because it accepts on faith the principle that all morals are relative. This violates, in tax-supported education, the Judeo-Christian moral principles of the great majority of Americans.

The educationists admit this. Paul Haubner, an Inquiry Specialist for the NEA, said at an NEA conference that the school cannot allow parents to influence the kind of values-education their children receive in school:

> That is what is wrong with those who say there is a universal system of values. Our [humanistic] goals are incompatible with theirs. We must challenge values.[5]

Underline this in red pencil: *The only absolute truth in modern humanistic education is that there are no absolute values. All values must be questioned—especially home- or church-acquired values.* Discard the experience gained from thousands of years of Western civilization. Instead, treat the students as primitive savages in the area of values. Let them select their own from slanted, inadequate information.

Nothing, absolutely nothing, is certain. There are no universal rules—absolutely none. Reflect on this paragraph from a world history text:

Modern physics teaches us that there are no rules that apply everywhere under all circumstances. Nothing seems certain anymore. If the universe cannot be fully comprehensible to us, how much less certain must we be about our theories of human nature, government, history, and morality? If scientists must be cautious in formulating theories about nature, how much more cautious and tentative must we be in framing conclusions about humans and their society?[6]

Physics is dragged into a world history text to say we cannot be certain about morality. The text cites quantum theory, itself a tentative field of study, as a speculative point of departure for pontificating about morality.

We didn't teach our three sons in this manner. We schooled them in honesty, fidelity in marriage, responsible parenthoood, and other virtues our society considers normal and right. We never said, as some textbooks do, "Make up your own mind about whether it's right or wrong to steal, or to sweet-talk a girl into sex." We've asked school administrators and teachers who sanction permissive teaching in the classroom if they tell their children that there are no definite rights and wrongs. We've never found one who would admit they personally followed these books' teachings with their own children.

The Lessons of Relativism
One way to decide if an action is right or wrong, the textbooks say, is to consider its ethics or expected consequences in a given situation. Joseph Fletcher coined the term "situation ethics" to convey this concept in a talk given to alumni at the Harvard Divinity School in 1964. As a professor at the Episcopal Theological Seminary, Fletcher had decided that Christian doctrine was "weird and utterly untenable" and so "de-Christianized" himself. Along with Christianity, he rejected all ideologies.[7] Dr. Fletcher later argued that rules must be justified by their relevance to perceived human benefit in any situation where a decision is necessary.

The situationists admit only that people hold to individual values and to group—or shared—values. According to the doctrine of Fletcher and other Humanists, all values are situational. That is, the situation determines what's right or wrong, and since situations constantly change, what's right today may be wrong tomorrow.

"Cultural (or sociological) relativism" and "ethical relativism" are code words in education for philosophies closely akin to situation ethics. Cultural relativism simply states that different societies and cultures hold to different values and morals. Students constantly are bombarded with this. Schools seem to spend more time exposing kids to different cultures than on training them in skills. A sixth-grade social studies Teacher's Edition emphasizes:

> Stress that whether a specific action is right or wrong depends on the meaning that a given group attaches to the action.[8]

This text does not distinguish between mere social conventions, and basic moral laws.

Ethical relativism supposes that differing moral codes are equally valid. The particular morals of the Netsilik Eskimos—who practice infanticide and wife-swapping—are as correct for them as traditional morals are for Americans.

Morals also aren't important. How the society views an action is. This is illustrated by a sex-ed text:

> In a society where values are constantly shifting, the young adult may often be confused by which set of values he or she is to follow.[9]

The value of a value is in the eye of the beholder(s). No one has the right to dictate his values to another, not even parents to their preadolescent children. That's the way "progressive" educators want to indoctrinate our kids in humanistic schools.

Drug education programs also suffer from the relativism taught in textbooks. In one book we've seen, teachers are instructed to:

> Divide the class into five or six groups and let them spend about ten minutes on this question. Should barbiturates be used by someone as a recreational drug? List the precautions that should be taken. What emotional condition should the user be in when using the drugs?[10]

This implies that recreational use of barbiturates may be acceptable under some circumstances, with the students determining the "situation." The text defines no "precautions" or "emotional conditions" proper to "recreational drug" use. This type of student activity will likely cause even more drug use.

A health text offered for adoption in Texas in 1982 devoted seven pages to discussing the harmful effects from the misuse and abuse of over-the-counter and prescription drugs, coffee, tea, and cola, while giving only thirty-nine lines to marijuana. Ten of these lines actually tell how marijuana might be helpful.[11] Texas officials refused to accept twenty-five of these health books until their drug chapters were improved.

If moral or ethical relativism continues to be taught unchecked in America's schools, we will drift first into anarchy, then into a totalitarianism. And we, who protest relativism in textbooks, are the ones who are compared to the Nazis!

The Real Intolerance

Actually, it is the Humanists who do not live up to their professed neutrality toward cultures and groups. For instance, textbooks seem to miss no opportunity to slur Christianity. Some world history texts treat missionaries as "bad guys":

> For many years men of the Occident have been preaching the religion of Dato (Christianity) and deceiving the public. . . . The religion of Jesus deserves all our hatred.[12]

Christianity also is described as having a negative influence on pagan cultures. Take this brief passage:

> When the missionaries preached the Gospel to me, I almost always got tired, and often felt sick in my stomach and wanted to vomit.[13]

High school sociology texts project a similar anti-Christian bias:

> Christianity . . . didn't help the blacks to gain dignity and equality in America, for Christian love was the whites' love of themselves and of their own race.[14]

"Diversity" to humanistic educators means ignoring or distorting all viewpoints but their own. It means censoring from the curriculum the Judeo-Christian values which a large majority of Americans hold.[15] That, as Cal Thomas wisely observes, amounts to Orwellian "doublethink."[16]

Values Clarification
In educational jargon, the undermining of Judeo-Christian ethical norms is accomplished through a process called "values education." The best-known aspect of values education is "values
clarification," or VC; its "bible" is *Values Clarification: A
Handbook of Practical Strategies for Teachers and Students.*[17]
   Dr. Sidney Simon, the book's principal author, claims that a
value is not genuine unless it fulfills seven conditions. A value
must be:

   (1) Freely chosen
   (2) Chosen from alternatives
   (3) Chosen after careful consideration of the consequences
       of each alternative
   (4) Prized or cherished
   (5) Publicly affirmed
   (6) Acted on
   (7) Acted on regularly

   These "strategies" for developing values are woven into nearly every school textbook—from social studies to sex education
texts. Not all of the strategies are presented in one chapter, or
in any necessary order; but all of them are components in most
books.
   Here's an example from a student's third-grade social studies
text:

   After you decide what you value, ask your parents what
   they value. Do you and your parents value the same
   things? Why or why not?[18]

The Teacher's Edition advises:

   Some children may use these [strategies] to strike out at
   parents; they can be helped by such questions as, "Do you
   think your parents really value money for itself?" or "Do
   you think it's parties they really value, or is it having
   friends around them?"[19]

Here's how values-education is handled in a fifth-grade social
studies text. The students are asked to agree or disagree with
these value-laden statements:

(1) It is important to work hard so you can make something of yourself. . . .

(4) You should tell the truth at all times.

(5) You should never say or do things that might hurt other people's feelings. . . .

(7) Having a new car and a big house and being able to buy expensive things are what people should work for. . . .

(11) If a man owns something, he should have the right to do whatever he wants with it. Nobody has the right to tell him how and when to use it. . . .

(13) The whole community has a right to tell a man what he is allowed to do with his property, and what he is not allowed to do with it.

(14) Stealing is bad. . . .

(17) Going to war makes a nation strong and great. War brings out the best in people and nations.

After the students state their convictions, they are asked:

Now compare your feelings about these statements with the feelings of the other students in your classroom. Are there some ideas that nearly all the students feel the same way about? If there are, can we say they are some of the values of your class?[20]

The student "convictions" are determined on the basis of situation ethics and peer pressure. The teacher is instructed:

Let each pupil decide for himself how he feels about each. Emphasize that this is not a test, and there are no "right" or "wrong" answers.[21]

Let's look at something a bit more complicated. A book called *World Cultures* for grades 7-12 consecutively follows the seven strategies of Values Clarification.[22] In this text the student:

(1) Judges for himself the merits of cultural lifestyles—including polygamy, witchcraft, political cultism, and ceremonial mutilation;

(2) Examines a multiplicity of sharply clashing cultural lifestyles clinically presented in a value-free narrative;

(3) Acquiesces to the inevitability of changing values;

(4) Ranks in descending order the ten values he most prizes in three categories;

(5) Affirms orally or in writing the desirability of changing values;

(6) Responds to the premise that, since one's cultural values determine social roles, changing cultural values necessarily change the social roles individuals play; and

(7) Reiterates the necessity and desirability of changing social roles and values.

Our associate, Professor Neal Frey, calls *World Cultures* "a piece of intellectual rape that aims to completely strip the student of any vestige of Judeo-Christian values."

"Homework" for such activities includes having students keep diaries on the activities of their parents and neighbors. Many parents have angrily observed that this amounts to a shameless invasion of privacy. But questions about personal and private activities in the home still appear in these books. We object strenuously to this. Besides invading family privacy, the texts require children to form values apart from the home and foster rebellion against parents. The term "values clarification" is now taboo in some areas because it has become a "red flag" word to many parents. But the strategies remain deeply imbedded in the curriculum.

Declining Skills

The doctrine of "no absolutes" also is harmful to the learning of basic skills. It works against discipline and commitment. It lowers restraints and makes it easier for students—especially those who do not have strong moral underpinnings provided by home and faith—to drift into destructive habits. It tends to stir up family conflicts with parents, as students feel free to choose values independent of their parents. As one teacher's manual observes:

> *Note:* Please refrain from moralizing of any kind. Students may indeed "tune out" if they are subjected to "preachy" talk about "proper English" and the moral obligation to "do one's best" in class and to "lend a hand" to the underdog in a battle.[23]

That's from the teacher's manual of a book adopted in Texas for twelfth-grade students with a very low reading level. It's intended to accommodate kids who have been promoted to higher grades even though they could not read.

We've already noted the tragic downswing in literacy (reading, spelling, vocabulary, grammar, and writing). Dr. Robert McGee of the Denton, Texas school system states the connection between illiteracy and "progressive" education very well:

> Too many teachers and administrators . . . are convinced "that reading and written expression are outmoded, that logical thought is pretentious, and that one can acquire all of the data one really needs through visual means."[24]

An overused word in textbooks is "communication." Some books stress that students need only to know *how* to communicate. In 1983, an instructor at a language communication workshop for teachers in Texas said, "It's grammar out—communicating in!"

Earlier, a curriculum director from one of the large county school systems in Texas called us for information about language grammar books. That was a year when dialects were in style; teachers weren't supposed to inflict grammar on minority children. If they spoke Appalachian, then "fur" was just as correct as "far." The curriculum director was very concerned by this fad, which, thankfully, has passed in many schools. Said she, "I would very much like for our schools to return to traditional grammar. However, I do not have a single teacher in my system who could teach it if we had it. It isn't necessarily their fault," she continued. "The education courses in the colleges are not training teachers in traditional grammar. In fact, most of my teachers wouldn't know a verb from an adverb or a noun from a pronoun."

Some textbooks tell the teacher to ignore grammatical mistakes and incorrect speaking and writing. Here's an activity where first-grade students are to describe the differences between three goats. If a student says, "The bottom goat is more bigger than the middle goat," the teacher is instructed:

> Do not correct the grammar that you hear in the children's statements. Instead, listen for individual differences. When you have several, write them on the chalkboard. . . .Explain that people talk and write in different ways and that these sentences are an example. You should not suggest that either example is "right" or "wrong."[25]

In the 1983 textbook adoption hearings, our State Board of

Education required texts to teach grammar rather than mere "communication"; as a result, our state now has greatly improved language-composition texts.

Learning to Read: The Case for Phonics

Before a student can learn correct grammar, he obviously must learn how to read. Traditional phonics—learning to read by sounding out letters and blends of letters in order to read the word—went out the window in favor of "look-say" reading—where students supposedly learn to read by memorizing "whole" words or by associating words with pictures. When reading scores dropped and parents complained, the educationists produced "eclectic readers," which add just enough piecemeal phonics to the "look-say" method to dupe the layman.

We've long been disturbed about such educational malpractice. Poor reading skills stunt vocabulary growth, which in turn stunts communication skills. In 1974 we found out that college-level texts were being rewritten at eighth- and ninth-grade levels to accommodate freshmen who had graduated from high school but couldn't master the college texts. Expressing his concern about this problem, columnist Vermont Royster wrote:

> The most learned of men are reduced to the level of children when they are deprived of commonly understood words and sentence structure; they can communicate only the simplest of ideas, and even those in uncertain fashion. The plain truth is that without language we can neither learn nor think. And those to whom written language is a mystery find, like some primitive people, that the world itself is a mystery. . . . It's discouraging to see what we do to ourselves when we cheat our young of the tools of thought.[26]

It is known that by imposing look-say teaching techniques on an alphabetic writing system, one can artificially induce dyslexia, thereby creating a learning block or reading neurosis.

> Reading disability is a form of behavior disorganization induced by the look-say method, because look-say sets up two mutually exclusive tendencies: the tendency to look at written English as an ideographic system, like Chinese, and the tendency to look at written English as a phonetic system because it is alphabetic. The alphabetic system is in harmony with the spoken language because it is based

on it. But the ideographic look-say system is in opposition to the spoken language because it is an entirely separate system of graphic symbols with no direct relation to any specific spoken language. Arabic numbers are a perfect example of such a system, because they can be read in any language. But numbers, when spelled out alphabetically in a particular language, can only be read in that language. In look-say, the written word is treated as a picture that can be interpreted by the reader in any way he or she wishes. It doesn't matter if the child reads the written word "horse" as "pony"—or, for that matter, "hundred" as "thousand"—for he's getting the meaning! Artificially induced dyslexia is today the most common learning disability in the United States. And that is why in the Soviet Union, *look-say is not taught*. Soviet children are taught to read by intensive phonics, the very method advocated by Rudolf Flesch and opposed by . . . the look-say establishment. The behaviorist educators have always known that artificially induced dyslexia could be eliminated overnight by switching the primary school back to intensive phonics. . . . If literacy is ever to gain ascendancy in the United States, it will have to be done outside the public education system which is totally controlled by the behaviorists.[27]

In 1980, "eclectic" textbooks were adopted in our state. In response, we simply asked that at least one or two of the series be based on a pure phonics method of teaching. We soon found we had disturbed a virtual hornet's nest. Norma and staff member Sheila Haralson were grilled and cross-examined for eight and a half hours because they had the audacity to question the professional educators' recommendations. In spite of our efforts, the State Textbook Committee recommended only those reading series using the "eclectic" method. However, this action caused such an outcry across Texas that the state Commissioner of Education received over 1,000 letters from parents, teachers, and administrators asking that schools be given a "freedom of choice" in selecting reading teaching methods. The 1,100 school districts in Texas also were polled to determine whether they were interested in using intensive phonics texts. The response was surprising. Sixty-five percent wanted the intensive phonics texts made available. As a result, the State Board of Education called for a supplemental adoption to provide five alternate reading texts using genuine phonics. This was a great victory for students and parents who want students to learn to read well.

Later, the Texas Board of Education mandated that two or more of the supplementary reading series to be adopted in 1985 must be geared to genuine intensive phonics.

A Nation of Nonreaders

During the time we were under attack, we remembered what Dr. B.E. Masters told Norma years ago:

> We are becoming a nation that does not read. Those who do not read do not think. Those who do not think will have their thinking done for them.[28]

A former state Commissioner of Education told me that, to the best of his knowledge, *every* educator involved in the teaching of reading in the state's central educational bureaucracy was anti-intensive phonics. At the time, we didn't realize that the incompetent teaching of reading was such a vested interest to educational "change agents." However, their efforts in this area may prove to be their Achilles' heel. We were to learn later from author Samuel Blumenfeld that:

> Never have we had more reading experts, remedial specialists, and doctors of education devoted to reading. Never has more money been poured into reading "research," and never have we had more illiteracy affecting every level of society. Several years ago, Prof. Steven Marcus of Columbia University wrote: "What we are confronted with in higher education in America is a situation of mass functional illiteracy. The situation itself is not entirely new, but the scale is unprecedented. . . . Hence, one of the historical functions of the first two years of higher education in America has been, and remains, reparative." This is the depth to which American literacy has fallen, thanks to the NEA and its friends. What is even more shocking is that reading disability has now been classified as a handicap like deafness and blindness under a previously unheard of category called "learning disabled."[29]

The Truth about Illiteracy

For the NEA and the educational establishment, massive functional illiteracy has proven to be the greatest financial boon in the history of public education. It has inspired such multimillion- and billion-dollar programs as Title One, the National Right to Read Effort, the Office of Basic Skills, Head Start, Follow Through, Special Education, and an unending flow of federal grants into "research" on reading—as if the teaching of reading were a mysterious, unknown process recently discovered by professors of education. When will it all end? If the NEA gets its way—never![30]

We recently spoke at a university in the state of Washington. A young teacher objected loudly to what we said about phonics. Norma asked her, "Have you ever tried teaching phonics?"

"No," she replied.

"Were you trained in college to teach phonics?"

"No."

"Well," Norma asked, "would you be willing to take some training and try phonics?"

"Certainly not," she grumped, as if that ended it.

Norma looked her straight in the eye. "Young lady, I can't understand why you are beefing. You don't know. You don't want to know. You aren't willing to give phonics a chance."

End of interchange.

Advocates of the "eclectic method" of reading have been indoctrinated against phonics. Like that young teacher, they've made up their minds. They will not give phonics a chance.

Many educators seem not to care that intensive phonics would cure most "reading disability." Their blind commitment to inferior "eclectic" reading shields many "reading specialists" from reality. Criticism of "eclectic" reading upsets them because it threatens their *status*. Such educators seem more interested in *professionalism* than in *education*.

Well-developed vocabularies are essential for success. But if students are not properly taught reading and grammar, where will they develop their vocabularies?

The Human Engineering Laboratory has found from many years of testing that:

> The one thing successful people have in common . . . [is] high vocabulary, and it's within everybody's reach. . . . Vocabulary will determine how high they climb. Right now, the present generation is heading downwards. Young people know fewer words than their fathers. That makes them know less. . . . Brilliant aptitudes aren't worth much without words to give them wings.[31]

They also found that:

> The recent rise in violence correlates with the drop in vocabulary. Long testing has convinced us that crime and violence predominate among people who score low in vocabulary. *If they can't express themselves with their tongues, they'll use their fists.* (Emphasis ours)[32]

What Next?

Much more could be said against the permissive cultural relativism and "values clarification" so dear to Humanists. Our mail, telephone calls, and audience responses indicate that parents have just about had it with such claptrap.

A friend mailed us a cartoon from a California newspaper which illustrates the stupidity of this methodology. The first panel shows a teacher holding a textbook entitled "Situation Ethics," while a little boy aims his slingshot at a girl in pigtails. As the teacher lectures on about relativistic ethics, the boy lets go and cracks the girl in the head with a hard object.

Hearing the girl's cry, the teacher stops and scolds him. "Now that was dangerous, Johnny! You could've put Mary's eye out! How does that make you feel now?"

Holding out his hands in mock innocence, little Johnny asks, "Relative to what?"[33]

There has to be a better way than leaving children adrift in a sea of moral relativity. As Professor Elshtain at the University of Massachusetts states:

> Education should be an education to character and citizenship . . . [in the belief] human beings have duties and responsibilities for their communities and that, to meet this challenge, a sense of discipline and convictions of right and wrong are required.[34]

The bottom line, then, is this: If public schools aren't going to be a positive moral influence, they at least should stop being a negative influence. Teachers should stop telling students that there are no moral values in life. Our children don't need that type of "education."

Footnotes

[1]Substantiated by surveys including: Gallup, *Better Homes and Gardens*, Connecticut Mutual Life Insurance Co.

[2]"Flames over Austin," *The Dallas Morning News*, November 18, 1982, p. 16A.

[3]As documented in surveys including: Gallup, *Better Homes and Gardens*, Connecticut Mutual Life Insurance Co.

[4]*Macmillan Gateway English*, Teacher's Manual, The Macmillan Company, 1970, p. 41.

[5]Reported in *Christian Inquirer*, April 1979, p. 4.

[6]*Unfinished Journey: A World History*, Houghton Mifflin Company, 1983, p. 461.

[7]Richard Taylor, "Joseph Fletcher: The Father of Biomedical Ethics," *Free Inquiry*, Spring 1984, p. 19.

[8]*Around Our World*, Houghton Mifflin, 1980, p. TE 70.

[9]*Toward Sexual Maturity*, Steck Vaughn, 1973, TRM, p. 29.

[10]*Modern Health*, Teacher's Edition, Holt, Rinehart and Winston, 1980, p. T40.

[11]*Good Health for You*, Laidlaw Brothers, Grade 4, 1983, pp. 156-172.

[12]*World History Through Inquiry—Looking Into History*, Rand McNally and Company, 1969, p. 17.

[13]*World History Through Inquiry—Cultural Exchange*, Rand McNally and Company, 1970, p. 46.

[14]*Inquiries in Sociology*, Allyn and Bacon, Inc., 1978, p. 158.

[15]Substantiated by surveys including: Gallup, *Better Homes and Gardens*, Connecticut Mutual Life Insurance Co.

[16]Cal Thomas, *Book Burning*, Crossway Books, 1983, p. 21.

[17]Sidney Simon, et al., Hart Publishing Company, Inc., 1978.

[18]*Principles and Practices in the Teaching of the Social Sciences: Concepts and Values*, Student's Edition, Green Level 3, Harcourt, Brace & World, Inc., 1970, p. 106.

[19]*Principles and Practices in the Teaching of the Social Sciences: Concepts and Values*, Teacher's Edition, Green Level 3, Harcourt, Brace & World, Inc., 1970, p. 115.

[20]*Man and Society*, Teacher's Edition, Grade 5, Silver Burdett Company, 1972, p. 11.

[21]*Ibid.*, p. 11.

[22]*World Cultures*, Scott, Foresman and Company, 1977.

[23]*Macmillan Gateway English*, Teacher's Manual, The Macmillan Company, 1970, p. 28.

[24]Vermont Royster, "Thinking Things Over," *The Wall Street Journal*, December 4, 1974.

[25]*Communicating*, The Heath English Series, Teacher's Edition, Grade 1, D.C. Heath and Company, 1973, p. 5.

[26]Royster, "Thinking Things Over."

[27]Samuel L. Blumenfeld, *NEA: Trojan Horse in American Education*, Paradigm Company, pp. 130-132. (Available from Research Publications, P.O. Box 39840, Phoenix, AZ 85069. $7.95 plus $1.50 shipping.)

[28]B.E. Masters, Ph.D. (American History and Economics from Yale), Texas State Board of Education member from our district who had run for this office because of his concern about textbook content. Dr. Masters founded four junior colleges and held a law degree.

[29]Blumenfeld, *NEA: Trojan Horse*, pp. 127-128.

[30]*Ibid.*, p. 129.

[31]David Hawkins, "Young People Are Getting Dumber," *The Dallas Morning News*, August 26, 1971.

[32]*Ibid.*

[33]*The Dispatch*, Morgan Hill, CA, November 3, 1982, p. A9.

[34]Elshtain, "Copping Out on Value Judgments," *Tulsa World*, March 13, 1983, p. I-8.

CHAPTER EIGHT

MENTAL CHILD ABUSE

"Change" is the battle cry of "progressive" educators. Society, they tell us, is changing. Religions, governments, mores and morals—all are changing. Nothing is stable, permanent, eternal. No institution, idea, or loyalty ever remains static. Family, marriage, chastity, fidelity—all are being reshaped.

And what institution will serve to usher in these changes? According to these same educators, it will be our schools. In the 1980s and beyond, public schools will help children change, adjust, and move into the future. They will help our young people leave behind old lifestyles and beliefs to become more human and more humane.

If you doubt whether school curriculums actually can change student values, just read the shocking testimony of hundreds of parents who appeared at recent U.S. Department of Education hearings. Excerpts from these testimonies, which concerned implementation of the "Protection of Pupil Rights Amendment"—better known as the "Hatch Amendment"[1]—have been published in a book entitled, *Child Abuse in the Classroom*. In its foreword, we read:

> A remarkable real-life drama took place in seven American cities during March 1984. . . . More than 1,300 pages of testimony were recorded by court reporters as parents, public school teachers, and interested citizens spelled out their eyewitness accounts of the psychological abuse of children in the public schools. They related how classroom

courses have confused schoolchildren about life, about standards of behavior, about moral choices, about religious loyalties, and about relationships with parents and with peers.

These hearings explain *how* schools have alienated children from their parents, from traditional morality such as the Ten Commandments, and from our American heritage. These hearings explain *why* children are so emotionally and morally confused and *why*, in the apt colloquialism, they need to "search for their identity."

These hearings explain *what* children have been doing in their classrooms instead of learning to read, write, spell, add, subtract, and the essentials of history, geography, and civics. . . . These hearings speak with the thunderous voice of hundreds of parents who are angry at how their children have been emotionally, morally, and intellectually abused by psychological and behavioral experiments during classroom hours when the parents *thought* their children were being taught basic knowledge and skills. Parents are indignant at the way that educator "change agents," spending federal tax dollars, have used children as guinea pigs for fads and experiments that have been substituted for real learning.[2]

Change Comes to the Classroom
We first realized education had taken a new turn when we saw how different modern texts were in comparison to older versions. That was in the early 1960s. Our second awakening came a decade later, when the "new" social studies texts came to Texas.

It was at that time that we recognized exactly *how* education had changed: schools actually were striving to become laboratories for behavior modification experiments. That is, the schooling process was now intended to promote humanistic attitude and values adjustment, rather than to teach students basic knowledge and skills. Students were to be "freed from traditional thinking and believing."

We weren't alone in noticing this shift. Former educator and U.S. Senator S.I. Hayakawa warned the Senate in 1978 that schools had become vehicles for a "heresy that rejects the idea of education as the acquisition of knowledge and skills" and instead "regards the fundamental task in education as therapy."[3]

At first, we didn't realize why modern educational philosophy differed so radically from what we thought schooling was supposed to be about. Then again, we had never heard of Georg Hegel, the German philosopher whose theories laid the groundwork for this revolution in the public schools.

To understand the philosophical axle on which modern education turns, you must grasp Hegelian theory. Before Hegel's time (1770-1831), men generally acknowledged the existence of certain moral absolutes. Actions were considered either morally right or morally wrong. There was truth and falsehood, positive and negative, good and bad. Yet Hegel claimed that truth is never permanently fixed, but always shifting between two poles. It always is in conflict with falsehood, flowing into a synthesis where truth is forever elusive.[4]

After studying Hegel, we saw how "progressive" education could twist and turn and never be held accountable for its actions. We grasped the goal of modern education: to transform children from the old way of thinking (which distinguished good from evil) to the new way (where relativism was stressed). Or, to put it another way, education's new goal was to train children to believe that morality must ever be fuzzy and gray. As one school counselor described it, everything in life is to be considered one vast gray area.

Educators and psychologists boasted that the "new" social studies represented the wave of the future. Education would do more than supplement family values. Education would heal students of "bad" values, starting with the concept of absolute right and wrong. Public education would prepare students for entrance into a society that eventually would replace the family.

John Boyles, editor of the *Educator's Newsletter*, stated flatly:

> There appears no alternative to acknowledging that we have created a way of living in which public employees [i.e., educators] will perform a significant fraction of functions traditionally left to families. . . . Marx, and other theoreticians of social change—Lenin, Gandhi, Mao Tsetung—have all spoken of the necessity of destroying the traditional fabric of family life in order to accommodate the needs of society undergoing economic transformation [toward a socialist society]. [The time] is fast approaching when the schools will be acknowledged for what

they are becoming: society's agreed-upon vehicle for institutionalizing social change.[5]

The First Assault

The "new" social studies texts which incorporated this outlook first appeared in California. One Californian who recognized the warped goals of the humanistic educators was Dr. Joseph P. Bean, a member of the Glendale Board of Education.

The "new" social studies combined history, geography, civics, and economics for grades one through eight. Dr. Bean was not opposed to the new teaching methods—which included team teaching, flexible scheduling, and allowing students to move at their own speed. His concern was over the "new" texts' implicit endorsement of Hegelianism, which "rejects nearly every previously held belief about man and nature"[6] and which considers man an animal who can be conditioned and reshaped into the humanistic mold. Dr. Bean felt so strongly about the orientation of the "new" social studies that he resigned his position when fellow board members adopted this curriculum.

These social studies texts also borrowed extensively from Pavlov's behavior modification experiments on dogs and prisoners in Russia. Pavlov's research once had been applied in mental hospitals and prisons; now, through these texts, it would be used on public school children.

According to Dr. Bean, this subtle blend of Hegel and Pavlov allowed "mental clinicians" (i.e., teachers) to modify their students' behavior by employing:

(1) Problem-solving exercises without fixed ethical norms;
(2) "Open-ended discussions" without an adequate factual background; and
(3) "Educational diagnostics" to determine how well the children have been oriented.

Classroom discussions could touch on race riots, peace education, the draft, abortion, family planning, oil slicks, or anything else deemed *relevant*. The teacher-clinician would not seek factual answers, but promote discussions without firm conclusions. Content was unimportant. *Process* was all-important.

Dr. Bean observed that the "new" social studies apparently were designed to change the child through three steps:

(1) "Unfreeze" home-taught values and standards;
(2) Give the child "different standards and a different concept of who he is."
(3) "Refreeze" and "lock the child into the [new] self."

The more we read and heard about this new plan, the more our blood ran cold. We shivered when we learned that Humanist philosopher Ashley Montague had told 6,000 California school board members, "Every child in America comes to school 'insane' at the age of six because of the American family structure."[7]

Montague's statement clearly reflected his belief that traditional values render children "insane." To the Humanist way of thinking, then, education should promote students' "mental health" by weaning them away from such values.

Protest

These social studies texts came up for adoption in Texas in 1971. Sixteen publishers competed for the opportunity to provide books for the first through sixth grades. Only five series could be chosen, so, much was riding on the votes of the Textbook Committee. One publisher admitted that success for his series would be worth a net profit of $1 million.

The books, however, were as bad as Dr. Bean said they were. Therefore, our Bill of Particulars against one series asked:

> To WHOM does the child belong? IF students now belong to the State, these books are appropriate. IF students still belong to parents, these books have absolutely no place in Texas schools. The author clearly states that these books are designed to change the behavior, values, and concepts of the child, based on the premise that the teacher is NOT to instruct, but to moderate, and to "heal."[8]

The teacher's edition of this series stated:

> If the classroom does not heal it has no teacher, only an instructor. . . . For the children do not always choose their parents well, or their heredity, or their environment, or their proper moment in history.[9]

We proceeded to cite hundreds of objectionable passages. We

particularly opposed the texts' emphases on "healing" personality problems and "remolding" students in a Humanist image. We noted assaults on family life and invasions of privacy. In fact, we found that these social studies texts incorporated fifty different mind and value changing techniques. Several of them interrelated in such a manner that even an adult exposed to them would have difficulty holding to his or her present values.

Basically, the content of these texts share three common characteristics:

(1) No permanent values are included.
(2) Everything is questioned, raising doubts and instilling the concept that values are worthless.
(3) Change is emphasized until it seems that everything "needs" changing.[10]

We fought these books hard, and were treated rudely—almost contemptuously—by educators who listened, instead, to the author of a very popular series of social studies texts, Dr. Paul F. Brandwein. Dr. Brandwein, an educational psychologist, was brought to the hearings at his publisher's request to defend his books.

In reply to our charge that these texts contained little factual content, Dr. Brandwein stated—before the Texas State Textbook Committee—that a six-year-old child enters school with enough facts about the history of our country because he watches TV.[11]

Consider Dr. Brandwein's comments in a teacher's edition:

> Postulate, if you will, a child entering the first grade and subjected for twelve years to a "fact"-oriented, topic-centered course of social studies. At the rate at which knowledge is generated, perhaps very little will be "true" as "fact" at the time of his leaving high school, twelve years later. His "school life" would, in a sense, have been "wasted."[12]

Five series of social studies texts were adopted, none of them acceptable to us, and the textbook "rating sheet" we sent to all school districts in Texas so indicated. But we did catalog these texts with the least offensive series at the top of the list and the most behaviorally oriented series on the bottom. When local schools made their selections we were grateful that the series we objected to least sold the most copies in both Texas and Arkansas.[13]

The History of Change

This experience was our first major encounter with the "behavior modification" or "mental health" approach to textbooks. But we wasted no time in researching this problem thoroughly. To our surprise, we learned that educators had been talking it up for years.

In 1933, the editor of the *Monroe Evening News* asked his readers: "Are the schools of America to be used as a propaganda agency to mold public opinion . . . ?" He then mentioned that a government official had told him:

> The rugged individualism of Americanism must go. . . . We must expect to accomplish by education what dictators in Europe are seeking to do by compulsion and force.

The editor concluded:

> And the taxpayers, whether they like it or not, are to pay for having their children converted to those policies.[14]

Even at this early stage, social planners were looking far ahead of most Americans—who naively assumed that the school was only to instruct students in the knowledge and skills they required to become responsible and productive members of society. By 1968, a writer in the NEA's official journal could claim:

> The most controversial issues of the twenty-first century will pertain to the ends and means of human behavior and who will determine them. The first educational question will not be "What knowledge is of most worth?" but "What kind of human behavior do we wish to produce?"[15]

Another publication is even more specific. The National Training Laboratories, run by the National Education Association, defends the use of psychiatric methods on children who are mentally well:

> Although they *appear* to behave appropriately and *seem* normal by most cultural standards, they may actually be

in need of mental health care, in order to help *them change, adapt, and conform to the planned society* in which there will be no conflict of attitudes or beliefs (emphasis ours).[16]

As for the more immediate future, Harold and June Shane, educators at Indiana University, predict:

(1) An increase in nonschool and preschool programs outside the home.
(2) Medical and dental exams in school and "early referral to cooperating social agencies for treatment of psychobehavioral problems."
(3) A "seamless" system in which grade cards are "destined to disappear."
(4) Added educational dimensions in travel, camping, and sociodramas.
(5) Increased biochemical and psychological mediation of learning, with drugs "introduced experimentally to improve in the learner such qualities as personality, concentration, and memory."
(6) The teacher eventually will become . . . a learning clinician. . . to convey the idea that schools are becoming "clinics" whose purpose is to provide psychosocial "treatment" for the student, thus increasing his value both to himself and to society. . . . Faculties will include culture analysts, specialists in information input, curriculum input; specialists who work on memory bank tapes for instructional materials, biochemical therapists, early childhood specialists.

The Shanes also predict that a corps of educational and health specialists will execute policy which "will not only anticipate tomorrow . . . [but] probably will help to create it."[17]

How This Material Reaches Your School
What appeared in educational journals in the 1960s was put into practice in the 1970s. In 1972 the General Accounting Office said there were at least 80,000 current federal grants—costing probably billions of dollars—for research in behavior modification. The purpose of this research was to learn how to get people to do things without their knowing they were being influenced.[18]
The humanistic educational establishment has never tried to

hide its plans for our children. What they say today will be in the textbooks tomorrow. In the interim, they mount public relations campaigns to convince federal, state, and local elected officials of the wisdom of their plan.

Here's how it works. The educational social planners map out a program—say, to help "protected" middle-class suburban children empathize with the lifestyles and problems of the inner city. They send advance notices of this program to selected friends in schools and bureaucracies across the country. These friends write letters back to them, reporting a local ground swell of support for the program—regardless of whether such support actually exists. The planners show these letters to legislators as evidence the program needs appropriations. Funds then are approved and put in the pipeline. The program is operating before most parents even know what's going on.

MACOS: A Case Study

Pilot programs usually are the first step. From 1971 to 1978, $5 million was awarded from the federal budget for experimental educational programs designed to exploit student emotions and manipulate behavior.

During this period, most of the money was funneled through the National Science Foundation (NSF) to develop *Man: A Course of Study* (MACOS) as a model curriculum for future social studies.

MACOS was the brainchild of Jerome Bruner, a Harvard behavioral psychologist and a major architect of the program to "humanize" our children (that is, "cure" them of "unacceptable" beliefs in the Bible, God, and moral absolutes).

The NSF eventually sought a textbook publisher to develop MACOS under an NSF grant. After fifty-eight publishers rejected the program, the newly founded Curriculum Development Associates of Washington, D.C. took the job. Federal money paid for students' and teachers' books, professional films, and tapes of the lifestyles of the Netsilik Eskimo tribe of Canada.

MACOS was designed to show how fantasy and feeling could be injected into education. Said Bruner's colleague, Dr. Richard M. Jones:

> For if ever a course was designed to create special opportunities for engaging the softer, more precious reaches of

children's minds, it is *Man: A Course of Study* [MACOS].[19]

Through MACOS, students were to see the human species at its worst and best. The planners hoped that children (the guinea pigs of the school laboratory) would become aware "of the similarities that unite all human beings" and gain an appreciation for "the differences that can divide some human beings."[20]

MACOS—and any subsequent courses—naturally took an evolutionary approach. As Dr. Jones put it:

> Man's overarching distinction as a species is that he has been the instrument of a qualitative innovation in the proceedings of evolution . . . his use of language, his use of tools, his social inheritance of acquired characteristics, his cosmologies, all derive their ultimate significance from this observation.[21]

In plain words, the "new" social studies curriculum, with MACOS in the vanguard, was designed to promote a humanistic world view. This effort, of course, was financed with our tax dollars.

Fundamentally, MACOS assumed that life is wrapped up in atheistic evolution. No God. Just chance. No moral absolutes. Just different lifestyles in different cultures, all contributing to evolutionary change, all representative of the family of man—and none authoritative.

So how was the new "mental health" curriculum—with MACOS as Exhibit A—to deal with conscience and religious beliefs? Ponder this suggestion from Dr. Jones:

> If, as consequences in passing, some children develop personal qualities of conscience which render them somewhat less "slapdash" as "transmission receivers"; which enable them more often to test and reject and less often "to believe much too much and believe it much too strongly"; if . . . there is a secondary gain in mental health in some instances, I think we [psychologists and educators] should not feel burdened by thoughts of having perhaps practiced medicine without license.[22]

You may have to reread this paragraph several times to understand Jones' main points. He is saying that children improve in mental health when they come *to test and reject more, and believe less*. Plainly: the new manuals of psychotherapy for the classroom are intended to increase the "sanity" of children by attacking and undermining the "insanity" of religion and the family.

Dr. Jones' ideas are not unique. He simply is a representative of the new healers in the classroom.

But let's come back to MACOS, which was intended to be a model social studies curriculum. Through MACOS, children would be led to "step outside of their own cultures to question [home, moral, and religious] values they may have already learned."[23]

The course was self-contained. Students were to "discover" the new values exclusively in MACOS books, simulation games, and films. They could not look elsewhere. The teachers were to dissuade them from initiating any questions on their own. MACOS was indoctrination, pure and simple.

MACOS' Strategies

Let's look at some of the values adjustment strategies found in MACOS. One simulation game was designed to last for a week. It placed students in an Arctic environment where the object was to "capture" enough seals to stay alive. The victor could do this only by "starving" his co-players. A story about an old woman abandoned to die because she was no longer useful to society reinforced the Netsilik Eskimo method of surviving by killing.[24]

Through the use of films, tapes, readings, and various games, students also "discovered" such Netsilik values as cannibalism, infanticide, wife-swapping, and mating with animals. The students even could role play leaving people to die.[25] In one story used in this unit, a wife runs into the snow to escape her murderous husband. He catches her and chops her up with a bone carving knife, then slices the pieces and consumes her flesh.

Now suppose some little fifth-grader suggests that Netsilik ways are unpleasant. Suppose he mentions that the morals he learned in church and at home are superior to the Netsiliks'. Naughty, naughty. It isn't nice to show cultural imperialism, he'll be told. The Netsiliks are part of the grand scheme of evolution in which you too are involved. Who is to say one culture is better than another? Why, you probably do things the Netsiliks find distasteful.

The Fate of MACOS

MACOS was simply too much for some educators. One psychologist was quoted as saying the infanticide lessons "could do lasting harm to the children."[26]

Eventually, parental protests reached Congress. Former-Representative John Conlan of Arizona examined the materials and was horrified. Against the howls of liberal congressmen and educational lobbyists, Conlan led the effort which cut off MACOS' federal funding in midstream.

Still, MACOS didn't die a quick death. The program *was* continued in many schools and we still see excerpts from it in other curriculum programs.

When MACOS was being introduced in New Zealand, Norma was invited there to alert parents about its content. She also spoke in Australia, where MACOS already was in a number of schools. Her host for one series of speeches was Mrs. Joh Bjelke-Petersen, the wife of the Premier of Queensland. After reviewing material which Norma provided for her, Mrs. Bjelke-Petersen was astounded to learn about the content of this deadly American import. She passed the information about MACOS on to her husband. Parent groups, after hearing Norma, also protested to the Premier. A newspaper editorialized:

> There are enough elements at large in the community now trying to erode the role and status of the family in modern society without [MACOS] being taught in our classrooms as a course of study! Through MACOS, is the school to be the training ground for revolutionaries? Are primary children to be encouraged to believe "society is sick, rotten, and corrupt" and must be changed? Are teachers to forego the education process for "social engineering"? Are our children to be engineered into believing that aggression is necessary to achieve status and power in our society, as MACOS teaches? That is made abundantly clear in the MACOS indoctrination.[27]

Premier Bjelke-Petersen and his Cabinet ordered MACOS out of the seventeen Queensland schools where it was being tested. The president-elect of the Queensland Teacher's Union was furious at this action. He accused the Cabinet of setting themselves up as "the final arbiter of the education syllabuses." But Professor Rupert Goodman at Queensland University called the banishing of MACOS:

A very wise and sensible decision. . . . Perhaps the greatest concern has been expressed by psychiatrists and allied professional groups. They fear teachers have stepped over the thin line which distinguishes education from mind manipulation.[28]

Because it was *the* pilot program in this genre, MACOS' defeat marked a major setback for the educational elite. Not only did they lose the fight for MACOS, they alerted thousands of people to their real intentions. Publishers also felt the heat. The social studies texts presented in Texas after the demise of MACOS were far less objectionable than the previous ones.

The irony of all this is that *we* are accused of exercising mind control over the children of America. We are said to be against inquiry and investigation in education. Let us repeat, loudly: We favor honest inquiry when children are given sufficient information on *all sides* and allowed to develop their *own* conclusions. We want sound education. The new educational "change agents" want indoctrination on their terms with resource material cleverly introduced to manipulate students toward humanistic conclusions. This they falsely call "inquiry."

The Ongoing Battle

This doesn't mean the "change agents" have given up. They've just taken one step backward, biding their time until parents let down their guard. Of course, we're not speaking solely of the situation in Texas. Letters and calls from parents indicate that the educational establishment's "mental health" blitzkrieg is gathering speed in other states.

We suggest that you take a hard look at the social studies curriculum your children use. Get the teachers' books if you can. Do the books, films, and other aids heavily emphasize feelings and fantasizing? Are the students asked questions about family, neighbors, and religion which invade their privacy? Does factual learning take a backseat to behavior modification and attitude formation? Are your local teachers called "learning clinicians," or some similar term?

If the answer to these questions is yes, it's time to get "cracking." We'll be glad to help you. It would be foolish for you to "reinvent the wheel" when we have thousands of thorough textbook reviews. In preparing these reviews, we spend approximately two full weeks painstakingly and meticulously examining a given text. Our friends say they're great aids.

The new psychotherapists in education will surely not attempt another MACOS, with its episodes of murder, cannibalism, and infanticide. They'll simply go slower and be more subtle. One thing is certain, though: They're determined to put our children through behavior modification programs in those laboratories called public schools. The "mental health" they have in mind for our children is one that embraces the tenets of Humanism. In our judgment, this amounts to mental child abuse. Those of us who live by traditional, Judeo-Christian values should not let them force humanistic beliefs on our children.

Footnotes

[1]Public Law 95-561—November 1, 1978, Education Amendments of 1978, 20 USC 2701, "Protection of Pupil Rights," SEC. 1250. Section 439 (b), 20 USC 1232h.

[2]*Child Abuse in the Classroom*, Excerpts from Official Transcript of Proceedings before the U.S. Department of Education, Edited by Phyllis Schlafly, $4.95, Pere Marquette Press, Alton, Illinois 62002. The hearings were held in Seattle, Pittsburgh, Kansas City, Phoenix, Concord, Orlando, and Washington, D.C. on March 13, 16, 19, 20, 21, 23, 27, 1984, pp. 11-13.

[3]*Child Abuse in the Classroom*, p. 13.

[4]According to Hegel, the *process* of defining truth and virtue is always absolute; but the *content* of truth and virtue actually defined, is relative to the particular situation. Or, in Hegelian terms, "thesis" (i.e., temporary truths and virtues) eventually merges with "anthithesis" (i.e., temporary falsehoods and vices) into a new "synthesis" (i.e., new truths and virtues), and this "dialectical" process repeats itself over and over again. Old truths and virtues become new falsehoods and vices. Old falsehoods and vices become new truths and virtues. Hegel, of course, was a strong statist, and held that the state defined what was true and virtuous at any particular time.

[5]Cited in *National Review*, "From the Academy," Russell Kirk, November 11, 1977, p. 1301.

[6]Joseph P. Bean, M.D., *Public Education—River of Pollution* and its sequel, *The Source of the River of Pollution*, Educator Publications, 1110 S. Pomona Ave., Fullerton, CA 92632.

[7]Cited from John Steinbacher, "To Capture a Nation—Change

the Religion," in *The National Educator*. As cited by Vince Nesbitt, *Humanistic Morals and Values Education*, pub. by Vince Nesbitt, 12 Beta Road, Lane Cove, N.S.W. 2066, Australia, 1981, p. 5, Dr. Montague told 1,000 home economics teachers in Anaheim, Calif., on Nov. 9, 1970, "The American family structure produces mentally ill children." Nesbitt also cited *Education to Remold the Child*, Parent and Child Advocate, Rt. 4, Watertown, WI 53094, p. 30, which quotes educators' views on the "mental illness" of children: "Dr. Pierce of Harvard University: 'Every child in America who enters school at the age of five is mentally ill, because he comes to school with allegiance toward our elected officials, toward our founding fathers, toward our institutions, toward the preservation of this form of government we have . . . the children are sick, because the truly well individual is one who has rejected all of those things and is what I would call the true international child of the future.' " pp. 5, 28.

[8]Exhibit 34, pp. 180-206, "Protests and Statements on Certain Books Being Considered for Adoption in 1971," compiled by Texas Education Agency, Bill of Particulars by Mel and Norma Gabler.

[9]*The Social Sciences*, Teacher's Edition, Harcourt, Brace, & Jovanovich, Levels 3 & 4, 1970, p. T-10.

[10]Educational Research Analysts, Form T-258.

[11]Texas State Textbook Committee Hearings, Austin, TX, September 14, 1971.

[12]*Principles and Practices in the Teaching of the Social Sciences Concepts and Values*, Harcourt, Brace & World, Inc., 1970, p. T-12.

[13]Educational Research Analysts, Form T-240, *Contemporary Social Science Curriculum*, Silver Burdett, 1972; *Focus on Active Learning*, Macmillan, 1971; *Field Social Studies Program*, Field, 1970; *Concepts in Social Science*, Laidlaw, 1972; *The Social Sciences: Concepts & Values*, Harcourt, 1970.

[14]*Monroe [Michigan] Evening News*, September 13, 1933, as cited in "Views from Other Newspapers—'And It Came to Pass,' " *The Shreveport Journal*, January 20, 1970.

[15]*Today's Education*, February, 1968. Cited by Mary Williams, "Big Brother in Education," Frederick County, Maryland Civic Federation, Spring, 1976, p. 2.

[16]*Issues in Training*, National Training Laboratories, p. 47, as cited by Vince Nesbitt, *Humanistic Morals and Values Educa-*

tion, published by Vince Nesbitt, 12 Beta Road, Lane Cover, N.S.W. 2066, Australia, p. 5.

[17]Harold G. and June Shane, "Forecast for the 70's," *Today's Education*, February, 1969, pp. 29-32.

[18]Paul Scott, THE SCOTT REPORT, The Washington News-Intelligence Syndicate, Washington, D.C., January 5, 1972, p. R-10.

[19]Richard M. Jones, *Fantasy and Feeling in Education*, Harper Colophon Books, 1968, p. 27.

[20]*Ibid.*, p. 211.

[21]*Ibid.*, p. 211.

[22]*Ibid.*, pp. 225-226.

[23]James C. Hefley, *Textbooks on Trial*, Victor Books, 1976, p. 113.

[24]Leaving "Old Kigtak" to die was included in two student's books and in two teacher's manuals: *Songs and Stories of the Netsilik Eskimos*, Education Development Center, Inc., 1968, student's edition, p. 43; *A Journey to the Arctic*, Education Development Center, Inc., 1969, student's edition, pp. 20-22; *The Netsilik Eskimos on the Sea Ice*, Education Development Center, Inc., 1969, teacher's manual, p. 18; Man: A Course of Study *Talks to Teachers*, Education Development Center, Inc., 1970, teacher's manual, pp. 101-102.

[25]MACOS, *The Netsilik Eskimos on the Sea Ice*, teacher's manual seven, Curriculum Development Associates, 1970, p. 21.

[26]Jones, *Fantasy and Feeling in Education*, p. 69.

[27]*The Manly Daily* [Australia], November 26, 1977, p. 2.

[28]"State Drops Course for Schools," *The Courier-Mail* [Brisbane, Australia], January 20, 1978, p. 1.

CHAPTER NINE

EVOLUTION vs. CREATION: WHERE THE BATTLE LINES ARE DRAWN

The press still calls it "Monkeytown, U.S.A.," this beautiful little Tennessee town which nestles in a green valley thirty miles northeast of Chattanooga. Though Dayton is perhaps best known as the site of the infamous Scopes "Monkey Trial," local folks are more proud of their plump, red strawberries, for which they hold a festival once a year. But that doesn't prevent tourists from inanely asking, "Do any monkeys still live here?" The patient locals simply grin and reply, "No, but a good many pass through."

We get tired of hearing about Dayton and the Scopes Trial too. Tired of seeing headlines that label present battles over the teaching of evolution and creationism new "monkey trials." Tired of telling reporters who should know better: "No, creationism wasn't outlawed in the 1925 trial. No, we are not asking that evolution be excluded from textbooks. We want evolution taught, but as theory, not fact. We want students to have the scientific evidence for both evolution and creation, then let them make up their own minds. No, not all scientists are evolutionists."

Dr. John N. Moore, who recently retired from teaching natural science at Michigan State University, is one of many university professors who believe that scientific evidence favors creation. He is the author of *How to Teach Origins (Without ACLU Interference)*.[1] Years ago he assembled a twenty-five page bibliography of recognized scientific books critical of evolution. That list undoubtedly would be much longer today.

No, creationists are not bigots. The real bigots are evolutionists who insist on censoring the evidence for creation and having the theory of evolution taught *as fact.* A woman reporter from NBC Television News—you'd know her name instantly—began her interview with us by saying, "Of course, we know that all scientists are evolutionists."

"Oh, that isn't true at all," Norma said. "There's Von Braun and Einstein and . . . "

She quickly cut Norma short: "Now, let's not get into name-calling."

So we continue to correct reporters, and school officials, and anyone else who will listen. Still we keep hearing the same old tired dogmatic pronouncements from people who seem fearful their cherished beliefs will be rejected.

We're assuming more of you. We believe you want to know what the fight over the teaching of origins is all about. We think you're interested in understanding where this conflict stands in the textbooks and schools today.

Let's start, therefore, with some definitions essential to understanding both sides.

Some Helpful Definitions

Evolution is a theory which claims that the Earth was formed by chance about 4.5 billion years ago. By a random process, evolutionists claim, chemicals in the seas evolved into simple cell life. This life then evolved—again by chance—over millions of years into every plant and animal that's ever lived.

Changes in life forms occur through *mutation* and *natural selection.* Mutation is a random and unpredictable change in the reproductive material—genes and chromosomes—of a cell. Mutations change genetic structure, but cannot increase net genetic complexity. Natural selection—or survival of the fittest—is nature's way of weeding out life forms which are less equipped to survive. Evolutionists claim that man is the result of one of these evolving and surviving lines. Unless he intervenes to change evolution, he inevitably will develop into a more advanced form.

Creationism is the belief that the universe, Earth, and all basic types of plants and animals, along with the first man and woman, were supernaturally and specially created by God. Creationists theorize that many changes in life forms have taken place since creation, but no basic type of organism has ever evolved into another.

Scientific method consists of "the collection of data through observation and experiment, and the formulation and testing of hypotheses."[2]

Belief is "a state or habit of mind in which trust or confidence is placed in some person or thing."[3]

A *hypothesis* is an assumption which cannot be fully proved due to an "insufficiency of presently attainable evidence"; it is, therefore, "a tentative explanation."

A *theory* implies an assumption which benefits from "a greater range of evidence and a greater likelihood of truth."

A *law* "implies a statement of order and relation in nature that has been found to be invariable under the same conditions."[4]

In light of these definitions, it's clear that evolution and creation really are hypotheses, though we shall use the term "theory" to describe both. Neither has ever been tested by direct scientific observations or experiments. No one was around to observe the instant at which life began. No evolutionist has ever replicated the supposed emergence of life from dead matter; nor has any creationist ever filmed, recorded, or otherwise documented the creation of something from nothing.

The Role of Inference

Neither theory, then, can be proved or disproved solely by scientific methods. The only evidence for either theory comes from *inferential conclusions*.

We make inferential statements all the time. We come home and see a puddle in our yard and infer that it rained recently. We weren't *there* to see the rain; the water could have bubbled up from an underground spring. Fortunately, we have neighbors who can tell us whether it actually rained or not. But no one living today was on the scene when the world began.

Of course, biblical records of this event exist. We accept this account as historically true. But we cannot *prove* the biblical account of creation by the scientific method. Nonetheless, on the basis of certain *inferential* evidences—which we'll examine later—we can theorize that divine creation is responsible for the world and all life.

Evolutionists, however, hypothesize that the Earth and cosmos developed by chance. Charles Darwin, for example, noted that members of a species compete both with each other, and with members of other species, to survive. He called the results of this struggle the "survival of the fittest," and compared them to man's scientific breeding of hardier and more useful plants and animals. Darwin might have inferred that genetic variations were a part of the master plan of a Creator. Instead, he inferred that living things had been evolving this way for millions of years with the fittest surviving and advancing ever upward. This theory—that natural selection is the process by which evolution occurred—became the "backbone" of evolutionary theory taught in textbooks today.

Darwin and other evolutionists inferred that if gradual evolution were true, the fossil or skeletal remains of transitional forms—ape-man creatures, for instance—should exist somewhere. Evolutionists, however, have not been able to find and positively identify a single one. Not one!

When unusual bones once were unearthed near Heidelberg, Germany, evolutionists claimed that they had found the missing link between man and apes. Artists drew pictures of an ape-man as they thought he must have looked. The pictures were printed in national magazines, textbooks, and displayed in museums. This bubble burst, though, when reputable scholars determined that the creature's jawbone was fully human. He was just another man.

Paleontologists digging in Nebraska found a tooth they speculated came from a missing link. Again, pictures were drawn and circulated. Testimony concerning "Nebraska Man" was even presented at the Scopes Trial. Sadly, for evolution, a chemist later examined the tooth and established that it was from an extinct pig.

The famous "Piltdown Man" turned out to be a hoax perpetrated by pranksters who buried the skeletal remains of several animals in a gravel pit.

"Peking Man" was heralded as the missing link for many years. But his remains mysteriously disappeared. "Neanderthal Man" was not an apelike creature either, as first thought, but only an old man who had suffered severely from arthritis. "New Guinea Man" caused quite a stir until a tribe of people were discovered just like him in an area north of Australia. "Cro-Magnon Man," uncovered in France, is now generally acknowledged to be indistinguishable from modern man.[5]

Still, the imagined pictures of some of these fakes continue to appear in magazines and textbooks as archeological facts.

As to the existence of fossils which contain transitional forms, Luther Sunderland, an aerospace engineer, interviewed experts from five of the world's leading paleontological museums. None could produce a single fossil or living organism which shows intermediate stages between the major groups of creatures. Every specimen in their museums had been found with all organs and structures complete.[6]

The Fight over Evolution

Evolution first met stiff resistance in the United States in the public schools, which were controlled by elected boards and legislatures. After Tennessee passed a law in 1925 forbidding the teaching of evolution in Tennessee public schools, the American Civil Liberties Union advertised for a teacher willing to test this statute. Businessmen in depressed Dayton saw an opportunity to put their town on the map and enlisted a local teacher, John T. Scopes, to help test the law. Scopes actually was a math teacher, but had substituted in biology class when the regular teacher was sick. He quickly coached his students to make sure they would testify he had taught them evolution.

When Scopes subsequently was charged with violating the law, evolutionists recruited Clarence Darrow, the most famous trial lawyer in America, to defend him. Creationists signed up William Jennings Bryan, a silver-tongued orator and former Democratic presidential candidate.

The trial became the greatest media event since World War I. Newspapers sent nearly 200 reporters to cover the case, most of whom already favored evolution. Best known of the lot was the acerbic H.L. Mencken, who termed Bryan "an old buzzard" and "a tinpot pope in the Coca Cola belt." The media had a hilarious time making sport of local hill folks and ridiculing fundamentalist Christians who were "ignorant" enough to believe in divine creation. One reporter didn't even bother to attend the trial sessions. "I don't need to know what's going on," he said. "I know what my paper wants written."

If more reporters had bothered to pay closer attention to the case, though, they would have told their readers that:

- Bryan had arranged to call Dr. Howard A. Kelly, the most renowned surgeon and medical professor in America, to testify for creation. However, Kelly was never allowed to speak; expert witnesses were not

permitted at the trial.
- Bryan and many other creationists were opposed only to teaching evolution *as fact.* "It is not the facts that do harm," said Bryan, who was a member of the American Society for the Advancement of Science. Rather it was "forced conclusions unsupported by fact." Evolution, Bryan said, "should be considered with an open mind" and its statements "fairly weighed. . . . All truth is of God, whether found in the book of nature or in the Book of books; but guesses are not science; hypotheses such as the hypothesis of evolution are not truth." Bryan said that the real issue of the trial was "the right of the people speaking through the legislature, to control the schools which they create and support."[7]

It has largely been forgotten that the creationists actually *won* the trial. This memory lapse probably is due to the fact that the state law eventually was changed to allow both creation *and* evolution to be taught as theories in Tennessee public schools. Yet we still hear reporters, educators, and scientists claiming that the Scopes Trial made it illegal to teach the evidence for the theory of creationism!

We believe the original Tennessee law was wrong in allowing only one theory of origins to be taught. But if members of the Tennessee Legislature were bigots because they passed such a law in 1925, then today's evolutionists, who insist that only their theory be taught in science classes, are bigots as well.

Evolutionists try to get off the hook by saying, "We don't oppose the teaching of creation. Just teach it in philosophy or social science classes." Their inference is that creation has nothing to do with science. We don't buy that.

How True Is Evolution?
Though evolution zealots like to believe that their theory is a proven scientific fact, the truth is, they sometimes get tangled in the web of their own propaganda. For example, TV producer Norman Lear's People for the American Way said in a recent press mailing:

Experiments can confirm the theory of evolution and give us confidence in its truthfulness, but they cannot prove the theory of evolution.[8]

How's that again? Confirm—but not prove?

Near the end of his life, Darwin himself admitted that he could not absolutely prove that any one species actually had evolved into another.[9]

Thomas Huxley, one of Darwin's supporters, called evolution "not an established theory but a tentative hypothesis."[10]

Loren Eiseley, an often-quoted evolutionist, wrote that "theories of living origins" have been postulated which cannot be demonstrated:

> After having chided the theologian for his reliance on myth and miracle, science found itself in the unenviable position of having to create a mythology of its own: namely, the assumption that what, after long effort could not be proved to take place today had, in truth, taken place in the primeval past.[11]

Evolution has been meeting severe challenges in recent years. Many leading scientists have thrown Darwinism completely overboard on grounds that the theory as currently taught in high schools and colleges is impossible.

These dissenters include world-famous British astronomers Sir Fred Hoyle and Chandra Wickramasinghe, and paleontologist Colin Patterson. Dr. Wickramasinghe, a Buddhist, even testified for creationism in the recent Arkansas creation-science trial. He stated that the possibility of chains of amino acids having come together to form life was infinitesimally small. Moreover, he said, such a process would have required much more time than the estimated evolutionary age of the Earth's 4.5 billion years. Stated Wickramasinghe:

> Contrary to the popular notion that only creationism relies on the supernatural, evolutionism must as well, since the probabilities of random formation of life (spontaneous generation) are so tiny as to require a "miracle" for spontaneous generation "tantamount to a theological argument."

Wickramasinghe also said that "his research drove him to believe that an intelligent creator" must exist. This conclusion was reached, he confessed, despite his "agnostic Buddhist beliefs."[12]

At a 1981 Symposium, Sir Fred Hoyle said:

The chance that higher life forms might have emerged in this way [through evolutionary processes] is comparable with the chance that "a tornado sweeping through a junkyard might assemble a Boeing 747 from the materials therein."

Hoyle further said that "he was at a loss to understand" the compulsion of evolutionary biologists "to deny what seems to me to be obvious [i.e., that evolution is not tenable]."[13]

Dr. Harold Morowitz, professor of biophysics and molecular chemistry at Yale University, testified at the Arkansas trial. He concluded that the odds of life creating itself, as evolution proposes, are one in ten followed by one billion zeroes. "The fact of the matter is," he declared, "we do not know the ways in which life comes about."[14]

Most of those who have rejected Darwinism have not become creationists. Instead, biologists have developed a new theory of evolution called "punctuated equilibria" or the "hopeful monster" theory. To escape the problem of missing links in the fossil record, they propose that change came very suddenly by huge mutations. These sudden, fundamental "leaps" in heredity produced new life forms that differed radically from their parents. But these "hopeful monsters" are just as elusive as Darwin's missing links, which were supposed to have evolved slowly over millions of years. Both share the same problem—no mutational change has ever been known to produce more complex heredity in chromosomes or DNA than was present before.

Many famous scientists acknowledge the truth of this fact. One such scientist is Pierre Grasse. He has been called "the dean of French zoologists," yet he rejects mutation-selection as a means of evolutionary change in scathing words. Mutations are "merely hereditary fluctuations around a median position; a swing to the right, a swing to the left, but no final evolutionary effect." He goes on to say that mutations "are not complementary . . . nor are they cumulative." That is, they don't work together, and they don't add up to anything. "They modify what preexists" . . . which means you can get no more from mutations than variation within type. . . . He strongly condemns attempts to use selection to salvage a few favorable mutations for evolution.

Directed by all-powerful selection, change becomes a sort of providence . . . which is secretly worshiped.[15]

Albert Szent-Gyorgyi, the Nobel prize winner, supports Grasse's findings. He believes that the chance of complex traits developing by random mutation has a probability of zero.[16]

The Reasonableness of Creation

Evolutionists of all stripes have been embarrassed in debates with creationists. In fact, many have become gun-shy of defending their beliefs in public forums. Typically, creationists stick to scientific evidence, while evolutionists ignore such data and charge creationists with trying to bring religion into the classroom under the guise of pseudo-science. Evolutionists also seek refuge in saying that since most biologists accept evolution, it must be true.

When evolutionists *do* try to present evidence for their side, creationists show how the same evidence can support creation. For example:

(1) *Similarity of living things.* Evolutionists say that the similarities between apes and men, for example, indicate that higher life forms evolved from lower life forms. Creationists hold that such likenesses are to be expected in the master design of a Creator.

(2) *Variation of living things.* Evolutionists contend that variations among life forms demonstrate evolutionary changes from the past. The fossil record of the horse is cited as a favorite example. Creationists say that such variations occur *within* basic types of organisms as they were created; but basic types of life forms *do not* change upward into more complex types. They merely change horizontally. Dogs, for instance, may change into different varieties of dogs; but they never evolve into cats or chickens.

Creationists and evolutionists agree that new species *can* develop over time from old species due to genetic variation and population isolation. This phenomenon is called "speciation." But evolutionists also term this process "microevolution." This is a mistake. "Microevolution" implies a net increase in genetic complexity, which results in new life forms (which is the core of organic evolution). "Speciation" does not denote this concept. Creationists must insist on this crucial distinction between actual "speciation" and alleged "microevolution"; otherwise, evolutionists will gain an undeserved strategic foot in the door. "Macroevolution," they will argue, is merely the sum of many small "microevolutionary" changes.

(3) *The fossil record.* Evolutionists believe the remains of plants and animals prove that life developed during previous geological ages. "Old" rocks preserve simpler fossils from early periods of evolution, while "young" rocks preserve evidence of more recent and complex life. Creationists can show, however, that the oldest fossils of any given organism appear in their present-day (or extinct) fully developed form. Fossils show no "links" between families, orders, and classes.

Creationists cite additional evidence to support this position. The law of decay (the Second Law of Thermodynamics) says every system in nature tends to move from order to disorder and run down—unless new energy and a design for orderly growth are introduced from an outside source. Evolutionists say this argument is irrelevant to evolution because the Earth is not a "closed system." They neglect to point out, however, that decay is going on in bodies *outside* the Earth. Several scientists recently have found that the Sun has been shrinking at a rate of about .01 percent per century for the last 270 years. At this rate, the Sun will vanish in only a million years.[17] This fact also argues for a young Earth; it means that in the relatively recent past, the Sun would have been so large and hot that life could not have existed on the Earth.

Evolutionists also insist the Earth is about 4.5 billion years old. Their main "proof" for this great age is radio-metric dating. But radiometric dating depends for its accuracy on several assumptions, one or all of which may be wrong, none of which are verifiable.

Generally speaking, for evolution to be valid, the Earth must be very old. As mentioned earlier, the random processes on which evolution is based would have developed over billions of years. Yet empirically testable scientific evidence suggests a young Earth. Dr. Henry Morris, president of the Institute for Creation Research, has compiled a listing of nearly sixty-eight examples that point to this conclusion.[18]

For example, the rate at which various elements such as copper, tin, lead, nickel, mercury, and silicon are washing into the oceans through the rivers of the world, compared with the percentages of these elements in the oceans, indicates that the Earth is much less than 4.5 billion years old.

Stellar dust is also settling on the Earth and moon at a known rate. If the Earth and moon were, as evolutionists claim, about 4.5 billion years old, there should be evidence for an accumulation of many feet of this dust. However, there is just enough moon dust to leave good footprints, indicating a young moon. Moreover, stellar dust is rich in nickel. If the Earth were very old, the Earth's crust should be rich in nickel, but it is not. Again, this indicates a young Earth.[19]

Creationists further emphasize the remarkable complexity of living organisms. The simplest one-cell life form is far more complicated than the most complex computer. To imagine that this cell developed by sheer chance seems wildly unbelievable.

Dr. W. Scott Morrow, professor of biochemistry at Wofford College, South Carolina, an agnostic evolutionist, concludes that the primary reason most scientists believe in evolution is because they "wanted to believe in it, they looked at evidence and saw it one way, and didn't consider alternatives."[20]

There is not space in this short chapter to delve more deeply into the inferential evidences for and against evolution vis-a-vis creation. The bottom line for both creation and evolution is how the world began. "The only alternative to a spontaneous generation [evolution]," says Dr. George Wald, "is a belief in supernatural creation."[21]

Evolution in the Schools

The first point of Humanist Manifesto I claims that the universe is "self-existing and not created." It should come as no surprise, then, that evolution is the cornerstone for humanistic educators. All inferences about man's nature and behavior begin with evolution. The late Sir Julian Huxley, a guru among evolutionists, defined a "Humanist" as:

> Someone who believes that man is just as much a natural phenomenon as an animal or plant; that his body, mind, and soul were not supernaturally created but are products of evolution, and that he is not under the control or guidance of any supernatural being or beings, but has to rely on himself and his own powers.[22]

Some evolutionists deny that textbooks teach evolution as fact. They say that there are no "facts" of science, only tentative explanations of available data. But evolutionists are not being altogether candid here. They really mean that doubt exists over the exact mechanism(s) of evolution. They do not doubt the "fact" of evolution itself. They merely question *how* it occurred, not *that* it occurred. Textbooks do indeed teach evolution as fact.

The big push for evolution in textbooks did not come until 1959, when the federally funded National Science Foundation provided $8 million to finance BSCS (Biological Sciences Curriculum Studies) for a new biological sciences curriculum to commemorate the 100th anniversary of the publication of Darwin's *The Origin of Species*.

The new books were designed for "inquiry-oriented instruction." Students would be asked to examine the evidence, ask questions, and formulate their own ideas in light of data they considered relevant.

Biologist Norris Anderson, as a member of the BSCS writing team, was excited about pioneering "inquiry education." He quickly found, however, that there was one area in which the inquiry approach was taboo—evolution. Anderson states:

> The problem faced by the BSCS became that of trying to produce materials designed to promote inquiry, and at the same time trying to "sell" the general public on the need to have evolution included in the curriculum. The result was a didactic rather than an inquiry presentation of evolution. Students were given only selected data to show the correctness of the evolutionary viewpoint, and no mention was made of the numerous problems with the theory. Unfortunately, this form of intellectual bias has been perpetuated in subsequent editions of the materials.[23]

Anderson's excitement over BSCS cooled, but he went along with the program because of "orders from above." But one day he saw a man coming toward him, arms dangling, grunting like an ape. Anderson recognized him as the writer assigned to prepare the human evolution chapter for one of the BSCS books. The writer hadn't found the slightest bit of scientific evidence to back up the evolution of man; he was told to present a case for evolution, nonetheless. This writer's odd behavior was simply his reaction to the absurdity of his orders. That incident, Anderson recalls, "began to shake my faith in evolution." Today, Norris Anderson is a spokesman for creationism.

The BSCS books—one emphasizing molecular, one ecological, and a third cellular biology—came to Texas in 1964 as the "Blue," "Green," and "Yellow" versions. Professor T.G. Barnes from the University of Texas at El Paso spoke against the texts as an expert witness. He pointed to an unbelievably dogmatic statement in the BSCS cellular biology text which declared "scientists had yet to find any facts in nature or in the laboratory that cannot be explained on the basis of the theory of evolution."[24] Dr. H. Douglas Dean, head of the Biology Department at Pepperdine University, cited a poll he had taken among high school students who had used the BSCS books. "Some of them were very religious," he stated, "some . . . not religious at all and I asked them . . . 'Did you get the idea that evolution is true or is it just a theory?' . . . 98 percent of them have gotten the idea that evolution was a fact."[25]

To our dismay, Texas officials accepted all three of the BSCS texts. *The Sweetwater Reporter* headlined: DARWIN DECLARED WINNER IN TEXAS "MONKEY WAR."

A Seesawing War

Texas creationists got a second crack at these evolutionsts' bibles five years later. They had a rough time, but this time only one of the BSCS books was recommended and adopted in Texas. In 1976 and 1984, not a single BSCS textbook was approved in Texas.

A major breakthrough occurred in May 1970, when the Texas State Board of Education required that "science texts must contain a statement on an introductory page 'that any material on evolution included in the book is presented as a theory rather than as a fact.' "[26] In 1974, the Board adopted a rule stating that evolution must be identified as "only one of several explanations of the origins of humankind."[27]

The Board's policy permitted—but did not require—the teaching of evolution. The status of creation science was not mentioned. The policy merely required the publishers to term evolution a theory; consequently, textbooks continued to include a considerable amount of evolutionary conjecture. Despite this fact, the evolutionists called the Board's ruling an "anti-evolutionary" policy and complained until, in 1984, the Texas Attorney General declared that this rule violated the First Amendment. The State Board then adopted a new rule which stated that:

> Theories must be clearly distinguished from fact and presented in an objective educational manner.[28]

Evolutionists first declared they had won. But some of them backed off when they realized that evolution must still be presented as a theory.

In Arkansas, creationists thought they had won a victory when the Arkansas Legislature passed an act requiring that creation science be given "equal time" with evolution in public school classrooms.

When this occurred, the American Civil Liberties Union took the Arkansas Attorney General to court. The trial was a travesty. The ACLU put 100 lawyers on the case. The Arkansas Attorney General gave the defense little attention, refused to deputize the most skilled creationist lawyers in the country, and declined to summon the best creationist testimony.[29] During the first week of the trial the Attorney General's staff asked shockingly few questions on cross-examinations, which caused the Judge to berate [him] for inept cross-examination. A Dallas newspaper that editorially supported the creation cause described the Attorney General's performance as the most "bumbling" and inadequate courtroom defense that its reporters had ever seen.[30]

Unsurprisingly, the judge ruled the "equal time" law unconstitutional. Despite the shoddiness of the trial, an ACLU attorney jubilantly told a news conference, "This decision has dealt the creation theory a fatal blow."[31]

Hardly.

A law similar to the original Arkansas statute has passed the Louisiana Legislature and is awaiting a court test. The Louisiana Attorney General says he will call the best witnesses for creation science and will secure the help of skilled creation science lawyers. If the case is appealed to the U.S. Supreme Court, creationists believe the Louisiana equal-treatment law will stand.

Fair Play

Teaching only evolution favors evolutionist religions. Teaching only creation favors creationist religions. Teaching either as fact is bad science. Teaching scientific evidence for one without giving scientific evidence for the other is bad science. The fair way, the scientific way, the constitutional way, is to define and present inferential scientific evidences for both models and let students decide.

Seventy-six percent of Americans say public schools should

teach *both* theories. Ten percent, according to a 1981 Associated Press/NBC News poll, want only creationism taught, 8 percent only evolution, and 6 percent are unsure.[32] A 76 percent rating is a pretty good majority for what creationists are asking.

A growing number of local school districts already are practicing fair play. Check with your school officials and see where they stand.

If they bring up the old censorship herring, cite a letter by Pennsylvania science teacher Robert M. Keener, published in *Today's Education*, the official journal of the National Education Association. It was written in response to an article by the NEA on "Censorship in the Schools":

> It is . . . contradictory for those who are against censorship to censor the teaching of scientific creationism. Any competent science teacher knows that the theory of evolution is not based on empirical science but rather on circumstantial evidence. Why not, therefore, present data that support creationism along with data that support evolution and allow students to make a rationally based decision? Teaching only evolution is censorship![33]

Most Americans agree that such an approach would be intellectually honest and scientifically acceptable. However, we're not asking that much of textbooks. All we're asking is that textbooks include scientific evidence *against* evolution as well as evidence *for* evolution, instead of presenting dogmatic assumptions and speculation.

Whenever scientists discuss a theory, they include evidence both for and against it. This practice is observed in all areas of science—except evolution. This suggests either that evolution is not scientific, or that evolutionists who selectively choose the evidence have something to hide.

Humanistic educators say they believe in democracy and fair play. Are they afraid that millions of young people, given a balanced education, will not become indoctrinated evolutionists? Evidently, they are so unsure of their position that they believe government force is necessary to shield students from scientific evidence against evolution.

Footnotes

¹John N. Moore, *How to Teach Origins (without ACLU Interference)*, Mott Media, 1983, 1000 East Huron Street, Milford, MI 48042.

²*Webster's Seventh New Collegiate Dictionary*, 1971.

³*Ibid.*

⁴*Ibid.*

⁵Bill Keith, *Scopes II: The Great Debate*, Huntington House, Shreveport, Louisiana, 1982, pp. 50-51.

⁶Report from Luther D. Sunderland, Apalachin, New York, January 1983.

⁷As reported in a scholarly update of the trial by R.M. Cornelius, "Their Stage Drew All the World: A New Look at the Scopes Evolution Trial," Tennessee Historical Quarterly, V1. XL, Summer 1981.

⁸Editorial Memorandum, November 1983.

⁹Charles Darwin, *The Life and Letters of Charles Darwin*, vol. II, D. Appleton and Co., New York, 1899, p. 210.

¹⁰Gertrude Himmelfarb, *Darwin and the Darwinian Revolution*, Doubleday, New York, 1959, p. 366.

¹¹Loren Eiseley, *"The Immense Journey,"* Random House, New York, 1957, p. 199.

¹²*Arkansas Gazette*, December 17, 1981, p. 9A; Bill Keith, *Scopes II: The Great Debate*, Huntington House, Shreveport, Louisiana, 1982, pp. 136-138; Dr. Norman L. Geisler, *The Creator in the Courtroom: "Scopes II,"* Mott Media, 1982, pp. 148-153.

¹³"Hoyle on Evolution" *Nature*, vol. 294, Nov. 12, 1981, p. 105.

¹⁴Bill Keith, *Scopes II: The Great Debate*, Huntington House, Shreveport, Louisiana, 1982, p. 126; Dr. Norman L. Geisler, *The Creator in the Courtroom: "Scopes II,"* Mott Media, 1982, p. 89.

¹⁵Grasse, Pierre-Paul, *Evolution of Living Organisms*, Academic Press, 1977 as cited in *What Is Creation Science?* by Henry M. Morris and Gary Parker, CLP Publishers, 1982, pp. 76-77.

¹⁶Gary Parker, *CREATION: The Facts of Life*, CLP Publishers, 1980, p. 76.

¹⁷Jack Eddy and Aram Boornazian, *American Astronomical Society Bulletin*, vol. II (1979), pp. 434, 437, cited in Shapiro, Parkinson, Dunham and Gribbin, *infra*; Irwin I. Shapiro, "Is the Sun Shrinking?" *Science*, vol. 208, no. 4439 (April 4, 1980), pp. 51-53; John N. Parkinson, *et al.*, "The Constancy of the

Solar Diameter over the Past 250 Years," *Nature*, vol. 298 (Dec. 11, 1980), pp. 548-551; David W. Dunham, *et al.*, "Observations of a Probable Change in the Solar Radius Between 1715 and 1979," *Science*, vol. 210, no. 4475 (Dec. 12, 1980), pp. 1243-1245; John Gribbin, "The Curious Case of the Shrinking Sun," *New Scientist* (March 3, 1983), pp. 592-595; Ronald Gilliland, *Astrophysical Journal*, vol. 248 (1981), cited in Gribbin, *supra;* and "Analyses of Historical Data Suggest Sun Is Shrinking," *Physics Today* (September 1979), pp. 17-19.

[18]Henry Morris and Gary Parker, *What is Creation Science?* CLP Publishers, 1982, pp. 254-257.

[19]Hans Pettersson, "Cosmic Spherules and Meteoritic Dust," *Scientific American*, vol. 202 (February 1960), p. 132; *Chemical Oceanography*, Ed. by J.P. Riley and G. Skirrow (London: Academic Press, 1965), vol. 1, p. 164 as cited in Dr. Henry M. Morris, *Scientific Creationism*, Creation-Life Publishers, 1974, pp. 151-155; and Peter A. Steveson, "Meteoritic Evidence for a Young Earth," *Creation Research Society Quarterly*, vol. 12, June 1975, pp. 23-25 as cited in Bible-Science Newsletter, July 1984, p. 15.

[20]Bill Keith, *Scopes II: The Great Debate*, Huntington House, 1982, p. 133; Dr. Norman L. Geisler, *The Creator in the Courtroom: "Scopes II,"* Mott Media, 1982, pp. 122-123.

[21]George Wald, "Innovation and Biology," *Scientific American*, vol. 199, September 1958, p. 100.

[22]"What Is Humanism?" The Humanist Community of San Jose, California.

[23]"Reflections of an Author concerning *Biological Science: An Ecological Approach*, BSCS Fifth Edition, Houghton Mifflin Company, 1982," by Norris Anderson, as submitted to the State of Alabama in 1983.

[24]State Textbook Committee Hearing, October 14, 1964, pp. 158-159.

[25]*Ibid.*, pp. 63-64.

[26]"Sensible Education," editorial, *The Longview Daily News*, May 6, 1970, p. 4A.

[27]This policy as entered into the Texas Register in 1983, stated: "(5) Textbooks that treat the theory of evolution shall identify it as only one of several explanations of the origins of humankind and avoid limiting young people in their search for meanings of their human existence.

"(A) Textbooks presented for adoption which treat the subject of evolution substantively in explaining the historical origins of man shall be edited, if necessary, to clarify that the treatment is theoretical rather than factually verifiable. Furthermore, each textbook must carry a statement on an introductory page that any material on evolution included in the book is clearly presented as theory rather than verified.

"(B) Textbooks presented for adoption which do not treat evolution substantively as an instructional topic, but make reference to evolution indirectly or by implication, must be modified, if necessary, to ensure that the reference is clearly to a theory and not to a verified fact. These books will not need to carry a statement on the introductory page.

"(C) The presentation of the theory of evolution shall be done in a manner which is not detrimental to other theories of origin" 19 TAC, Pr. 81.71, Subch. D, (a)(5).

[28]This new policy was adopted April 14, 1984 by Texas State Board of Education and entered into the Texas Register to become part of the Texas Administrative Code as "bureaucratic" state law as 19 TAC 81.71D, (a)(5).

[29]Bill Keith, *Scopes II: The Great Debate*, Huntington House, 1982, pp. 147-149.

[30]Dr. Norman L. Geisler, *The Creator in the Courtroom: "Scopes II,"* Mott Media, p. 217.

[31]Keith, *Debate*, p. 141.

[32]*The San Diego Union*, November 18, 1981, p. A-15, *Des Moines Register*, November 18, 1981, p. 8C.

[33]*Today's Education*, February-March 1981, p. 6GS.

THE BATTLE
FOR THE FAMILY

Thomas Jefferson once testified, "The happiest moments of my life have been the few which I have passed at home in the bosom of my family."[1] Yet today, a virtual war is raging over what constitutes a family—and who should control it.

As the first institution established by God (Gen. 2:24), the family is more basic than government or any other social institution. It is the bedrock of society. Empires have fallen when the family unit disintegrated.

But recently—perhaps because of the drumbeat of the mass media—some have doubted whether the traditional family has a future. This type of talk comes mostly from Humanist social engineers who want to abolish the traditional interpretation of the family, and from radical homosexuals and feminists, desperate for social and legal recognition of their perversions.

The enemies of the Judeo-Christian family have unprecedented power and influence in mass media, politics, and public education. They now possess a status which was inconceivable just twenty years ago. At this writing, practicing homosexuals are parading around the convention hall of one of our major political parties; and this party is acceding to all their demands—including their "right" to be the teachers and role models of our schoolchildren. Their most enthusiastic supporters at this convention, however, appear to be teacher/delegates and members of the National Education Association.

We are not surprised. We have seen wave after wave of textbooks attack the family, "unfreezing" children from home values and "refreezing" them by behavioral modification to embrace humanistic doctrines. But this brainwashing is not complete. The public schools have not been fully taken over. Thousands of us still are fighting for the rights of parents to control what their children learn. There *is* hope. But the hour is late.

Just What Is a Family?

The war against the family is fought in school textbooks on six fronts. The most crucial battleground involves the definition of "family."

Problems in this area can be traced back to Humanist pronouncements and policies. For years before the concept surfaced in public schools, radical sociologists were teaching that the "family" can mean any group that chooses to live together.

This teaching reached the public schools in the 1970s, when Humanist psychologists began saying the school must take over the training of children from parents. Using therapeutic teaching and counseling, teachers would now help students determine their values. Liberals cranked out congressional legislation that would have placed millions of children, whose parents Humanists deemed inadequate, into federally funded day care centers. President Nixon vetoed this bill on grounds that it would have committed:

> The vast moral authority of the national government to the side of communal approaches to child rearing over the family-centered approach.[2]

Nixon added that sound public policy should:

> Enhance rather than diminish both parental authority and parental involvement with children—particularly in those decisive early years when social attitudes and a conscience are formed, and religious and moral principles are first inculcated.[3]

This was a tremendous setback for Humanists who had been disguised as "family professionals." But they came back strong to support the three White House Conferences on the Family called by President Carter to celebrate the "diversity of families."

Pro-family people were disappointed that the White House had not defined the subject—families—for which the Conferences were called. But the Carter Administration was under intense pressure from the NEA and the National Organization of Women, both of which had supported his 1976 candidacy. In 1979, NOW had adopted the American Home Economics Association's (AHEA) non-traditional definition of the family. A family was:

> Two or more persons who share resources, share responsibility for decisions, share, values and goals, and have a commitment to one another over time. The family is that climate one "comes home to" and it is this network of sharing and commitments that most accurately describe the family unit, regardless of blood, legal ties, adoption, or marriage.[4]

At the AHEA meeting which adopted this definition, speakers urged that same-sex "families" be legalized, with legal guarantees of child custody for lesbian women living together. Said law professor Marjorie Maguire Schultz from the University of California at Berkeley: "Marriage needs to be redefined in terms of today's morality and today's attitudes."[5]

Typical Humanist mulch. Everything is changing and constantly needs redefining. Nothing is permanent. Not even the family.

Humanists tried to get their definition of "family" adopted by the three White House Conferences. They failed at conferences held in Baltimore and Los Angeles and were set back on their heels by pro-family delegates in Minneapolis—who pushed through the prevailing Judeo-Christian definition of "family," which stresses that families are established by heterosexual marriage, biological or adoptive parenthood, and kinship. But the Humanists succeeded in voting recommendations to increase government control over the home. As a delegate at the Los Angeles conference, I was not surprised to see the liberal "facilitators" manipulate the agenda.

The "New" Family and Textbooks

After the White House Conference, we looked for the new definition of "family" to start showing up in textbooks. It came to Texas in 1982. One homemaking textbook presented the Humanist idea at the beginning of a lesson titled "Your Family," with the initial explanation that a family is a "group of people living in the same home." The expanded definition tried to please everyone:

> A family is a unit or group which includes all those who live in the home. This group may include a father, mother, and one or more children. It may be a mother or father and one or more children. Sometimes relatives are part of the family group living together. Unrelated people can also form a family group.[6]

This Humanist-feminist-homosexual definition got shot down in Texas. State officials told the publisher to remove the words "a group of people living in the same home" and "Unrelated people can also form a family group," if he wanted his book on the list for Texas schools.[7]

Naturally, our opponents screamed "censorship." We reminded them that this, and other objectionable books, already had been censored of *traditional* values long before we saw them. A defensive publisher said his writers and editors merely were practicing "selectivity." We retorted, "You can select and publish anything you want, but we don't have to buy your book for use in compulsory public schools."

Replacing the Family

Changing the definition of the family is just the tip of the iceberg. On a second front, the authority of parents and family relationships is being severely undermined:

> The educational theorists, strongly under the influence of such humanistic psychologists as Carl Rogers, Erich Fromm, and Abraham Maslow, insist that schools must replace "incompetent" parents with therapeutic training in sexuality, values formation, death and dying, and decision-making, preferably integrated throughout the existing curriculum.[8]

Here is their rationale for this intrusion:

> Society generally has reconstructed itself so that it depends less upon the family or community groupings and more on institutions. Socialization used to occur primarily in the family, but the family has long since given over to the schools much of the task of preparing young people for

adulthood. Understandably, families have relinquished much of their authority in choosing the fundamentals of socialization to these institutions. We are educating as a society, not as family groupings.[9]

This represents the thinking and propaganda of those who want to monopolize child-raising and education. Parents are needed only to give birth, pay the bills, serve evening meals, and provide a place to sleep. With new techniques in fertilization and gestation, some say the time will come when parents will merely deposit their sperm and eggs at a clinic and depart.

We have news for the new child tenders. We know of no parents willing or wanting to "give over" their children to the school. A few parents neglect their children and shirk their responsibilities. Still, we challenge anyone to take a poll and see how many parents are ready to surrender their own flesh and blood.

At any rate, the homemaking texts submitted in Texas in 1982 tried to change the definition of "parents"—just as they also had attempted to alter the definition of "family." One text claimed:

> Mothers and fathers are not the only people who can be called parents. Teachers, counselors, and baby-sitters can also be thought of as parents.[10]

After loud protests, this definition was modified to:

> Mothers and fathers are not the only people who help others grow and develop. Teachers, parents, and baby-sitters can share the parenting role.[11]

In a summary section, this text originally had stated:

> Parents are people who care for and are responsible for the growth and development of other people. . . . [12]

This was replaced with:

> Parents care for and have primary responsibility for the growth and development of their children.[13]

This sort of thing is a constant battle. New books keep appearing with the Humanist definition of family and parents. Look at your child's texts. Where parents are alert and courageous enough to challenge the textbook adoption committees, the wording usually can be changed to support the Judeo-Christian view of the family.

But aren't school boards supposed to check books? Ha! Ask your board members if they read even one of the books they last voted into the schools. The professionals say, "We educators know best." That's good enough for most board members.

Most educationists believe they are better qualified than natural parents to care for and educate children. They think they can best help children discover who they are (i.e., social animals who can be manipulated and who can manipulate others), and form their values regarding morality, behavior, the community, nation, and world.

Of course, as we've often stated, children are given "selective" information. The educators call it "selection"; we call it "censorship." We repeat: such textbooks consistently censor Judeo-Christian and pro-parent viewpoints on religion, morality, and ethics in favor of Humanist arguments for animalistic evolution, self-autonomy, and self-fulfillment. This naturally works against the efforts of families who are trying to lead children to faith and spiritual commitment, train them to obey divinely revealed moral laws, and practice self-restraint and self-discipline.

No wonder Johnny and Jane are confused. At home they are taught one thing, at school they are led to question family mores and decide their own values. Psychologically, this causes frustration. Is it any wonder teenage suicides have escalated?

The professionals harp on the failures of natural parents. They beg for more government funding to hire more professionals to extend child care and education. They dwell on child abuse and parental irresponsibility. Yet they ignore the overwhelming evidence supporting the superiority of parental care over institutional supervision. Dr. Virginia Shipman of the Education Testing Service in Princeton, N.J., who has had years of experience in evaluating Head Start children, discovered that:

> *Only* when the parents of children in Head Start were
> deeply involved in *direct* responsibility for their children's

programs in daily activities did the children make lasting progress.[14]

The Hatch Amendment of 1978[15] forbids psychological probing of student beliefs and attitudes by the school in personal areas such as family relationships without prior consent of parents. Not many parents know that this law exists. Manipulative educators do not advertise it. We keep protesting such practices as presented in textbooks. It is an invasion of privacy to assign journal-keeping on parental activities. The school oversteps its bounds with questions about the affairs and activities of parents.

We declare that the school has no business causing students to examine or defend the values their parents have taught them. Where this happens, the offenders should be warned that it is illegal and must stop.

Educators' rights do not supersede parents' rights. The child does not yet belong to the state, and the U.S. Supreme Court has so ruled on numerous occasions.[16] Nevertheless, the attack on the family continues in the name of "we educators know best." Schools should provide academic training and never forget that children are the responsibility of parents, whose taxes support the school.

The Battle over Sex Education

A third front on which the family is under attack is sex education. In chapter 5 we documented the devastating impact of teaching that no sexual expression is inherently right or wrong, that sex is only psychological and physiological, that morality and immorality do not apply, except as the individual defines it. Textbooks seldom or never advocate abstinence, discipline, monogamy, and fidelity in marriage. It isn't nice to dictate morals in public school. You might offend those who have other sexual preferences.

National polls continue to indicate that over 75 percent of Americans believe in traditional sexual and family values. But studies by George Washington University researchers show that the elite of the commercial mass media hold far different values: 85 percent of this media elite see nothing wrong with extramarital affairs and 91 percent say being homosexual is OK.[17] These same researchers found similar value preferences among graduate students at the Columbia University Graduate

School of Journalism and among the movers and shakers in the film and TV industries.

Now, get this: In the area of sexual morality, American leaders—including educators—hold values that are much closer to those of the media elite than to those of the general public.[18] In other words, support for family and moral values has declined *most* among those in positions of influence over our children! Theorists and educational elitists have brought the antisocial sex attitudes of the commercial mass media into the school curriculum and now sponsor home-wrecking immorality.

Divorce and the Family

Skyrocketing divorce is a fourth front of attack on the family. In 1910, only one tenth of one percent of the nation's population had been divorced. That amounted to a total of 83,000 people. In 1982, 1.18 million Americans dissolved their marriages. The rate of divorce among professing Christians is almost equal to that of the population at large, according to researchers George Barna and William Paul McKay.[19]

Textbooks treat divorce as functional rather than dysfunctional; it's a normal part of family life rather than a tragedy to be avoided. A questionnaire at the White House Conference on Families asked participants to list ways in which the "divorce process" could be "improved." There were no references to the adverse effects of divorce on family members.[20]

Ample research shows the tragic effects of divorce on children. One study made five years after the divorces of 131 couples in the San Francisco Bay area showed:

> Thirty-seven percent of the youngsters involved were suffering from depression that was manifested in the following: chronic and pronounced unhappiness, sexual promiscuity, delinquency in the form of drug use, petty stealing, alcoholism and acts of breaking and entering, poor learning, intense anger, apathy, restlessness, and a sense of intense, unremitting neediness.[21]

Textbooks downplay the tragic aftermath of divorce. They present divorce, like abortion, as a therapeutic problem-solving device.

A homemaking text for grades six through eight calls the two-parent family "good" and "stable" and then commends one-parent families:

THE BATTLE FOR THE FAMILY

> The nuclear family structure can provide a good, stable setting for rearing children. . . . A one-parent family structure can encourage a high degree of sharing and a strong commitment between family members. The large majority of one-parent families are not planned. . . . This does not mean, however, that they are inferior. The one-parent family can perform the family functions.[22]

> In today's world, a blended family is simply another type of family structure. It can perform all of the family functions. It is no better and no worse than any other family structure; it is just different.[23]

> Others have a "till love do us part" attitude toward marriage. They see marriage as a short-term goal. They seem to expect that someday their love will come to an end. They plan to end their marriage at that time.[24]

Radical feminists have worked hard to liberalize divorce laws in their drive for unisex and "equality." The irony is that no-fault divorce has permitted many men to dodge responsibility for supporting their wives and children.

We favor equal pay for equal work by men and women. Thousands of women are the sole support of their families. Many married women must work to augment their husband's paycheck. The feminists claim these single and working mothers are their allies, yet polls and voting tallies for political candidates show that the majority of women in America—single and married—do not support the anti-family elements of the feminist agenda.

Changing Roles

The fifth front in the war against the family centers on sex-role changes.

Feminists have had the greatest success of any special interest group in changing textbooks. They have badgered publishers into adopting books which highlight the changing roles and responsibilities of men and women. The Macmillan Company says textbooks must do their part in "our search and struggle for a more egalitarian society."[25] As to accuracy, the Macmillan guideline declares:

> We are more interested in emphasizing what can be, rather than the negatives that still exist. . . . Don't show

"Mother bringing sandwiches to Dad as he fixes the roof." Show "Mother fixing the roof."[26]

Such "advocacy editing" has even turned off some honest liberals. *Washington Post* columnist Nicholas von Hoffman wrote:

> The guidelines claim that Macmillan wishes to eliminate "any traces of social bias." That in itself is fool's gold . . . what these people are selling is a depraved egalitarianism.[27]

Feminists blitzed Austin in 1972 by sending a platoon to bring the proposed texts into line. Their main goal: To eliminate the word "mother" from textbooks. Educational officials seemed to be of like mind and our State Board of Education went along. In 1973 we put out a press release, saying:

> This is an open attack on the heart of America. When was the Board policy changed to remove "mother" from all texts? After all, why should textbooks be rewritten to eliminate women as mothers, as though "mother" and "motherhood" had become dirty words?

In 1975 our state education bureaucracy preliminarily approved 2,274 changes in textbook content demanded by various women's groups. These included changing:

> "The man climbed the telephone pole" to "The woman climbed the telephone pole";

> "Mother will bake a cake" to "Father will bake a cake";

> "Father is coming home from work" to "Mother is coming home from work";

> "Mother sewed up the hole in Jack's pocket" to "Jack sewed up the hole in his pocket";

> "I will help Mother do the dishes" to "I will help Father do the dishes."[28]

By this time, the Board of Education was fed up with the feminists' unreasonable demands. In an overwhelming eighteen to-one vote, the Board refused to make 1,651 of the 2,274 suggested changes. This vote was a temporary victory for conventional sex-roles. Sad to say, most of the changes soon slipped into the books anyway.

These feminist-inspired changes cannot be said to mirror reality. Few women climb telephone poles; this is a job usually done by men. Such changes attempt to alter the real world rather than to reflect it. They are *prescriptive*, not *descriptive*. For blowing the whistle on these "change agents," we are called "censors." This tells a great deal about what "censorship" means in the Humanist lexicon. To Humanists, "censors" are those persons who interfere with the Humanist agenda.

We object to the radical feminists' propaganda against motherhood and homemaking. We oppose their campaign to erase the distinctions between husband and wife, mother and father.

Ponder this picture caption in a ninth-grade "homemaking book":

> Age-old reasons for fundamental role division are still exemplified today in "primitive" situations—women must stay close to home and children so they take on other jobs of homemaking; men traditionally leave home to provide for their family.[29]

We stated at the Texas textbook adoption hearings:

> Our country was founded on these so-called "primitive" situations which lasted over 200 years in that same tradition. Women's lib has changed this "situation." Unfortunately, since this change, we have experienced heavily skyrocketing rates of divorce, unwanted pregnancies, murder of unborn babies, etc.[30]

Homosexuals attack the family on a sixth front. As feminists strive to alter reality by equating sex roles, gays try to alter it by equating sex functions. Humanistic educators accommodate both with similar results:

> Vice is a monster of so frightful mien,
> As, to be hated, needs but to be seen;
> Yet seen too oft, familiar with her face,
> We first endure, then pity, then embrace.
> —Alexander Pope,
> "An Essay On Man," lines 217-220.

Fighting Back

We're called narrow-minded fundamentalists when we speak against changing the definition of the family. Yet unbiased surveys show that we are marching in tune with the values held by most Americans.[31] Why else are we having the influence educators say we are? Why else have we been interviewed by almost every network talk show and news broadcast in America?

We say, and we believe most American parents agree, that the onslaughts against the family in humanistic education are attacks on our national heritage. Humanistic educators use double-talk. They say "morality." They mean immorality. They say "family." They mean any group of people cohabiting, regardless of gender and kinship. The Hebrew prophet addressed these hypocrites: "Woe unto them that call evil good, and good evil; that put darkness for light, and light for darkness."[32]

In mock dismay, the Humanist enemies of the family exclaim that families need help, and then rush forward with more schemes to weaken families. Their ultimate aim, of course, is to phase out traditional marriage and family relationships.

We beg, we plead for you to awake and see what is happening to the family in America and in humanistic education. Two religions are in mortal combat for the souls and futures of our children and nation. One reverences God and the moral values of the Judeo-Christian Bible. The other rejects God and the Judeo-Christian basis of the American family.

We can avert the disaster that surely awaits us if humanistic educators win. We must reverse these trends. We must restore schools and textbooks to sanity. We must save our children. Not all at one time. Not all in one place. Not by denying our differences, but by working for common goals in our own communities and states.

We've demonstrated in Texas that changes *can* be made in textbooks, that better books *can* be obtained for our schools. You can do it in *your* schools. In the next chapter, we'll tell you how.

Footnotes

[1]*Five Thousand Quotations for All Occasions*, Lewis C. Henry, ed., Doubleday & Company, Inc., 1945, p. 86.

[2]William V. Shannon, "A Radical, Direct, Simple, Utopian Alternative to Day-Care Centers," *The New York Times Magazine,* April 30, 1972, p. 78.

[3]*Ibid.,* p. 13.

[4]*Family Protection Report,* 4 Library Court, S.E., Washington, D.C. 20003, January 1980, cited by Onalee McGraw in *The Family, Feminism and the Therapeutic State,* The Heritage Foundation, Washington, D.C., 1980, p. 5.

[5]*Ibid.,* p. 6.

[6]*Living, Learning, and Caring,* Ginn and Company, 1981, p. 12.

[7]Texas Textbook Adoption Changes and Corrections Requested of Publishers, 1982, p. 36.

[8]Onalee McGraw, *The Family, Feminism, and the Therapeutic State,* The Heritage Foundation, Washington, D.C., 1980, p. 2.

[9]*Proposed Sixth Grade Sex Education Program Majority Report,* Madison School District, Phoenix, Arizona, March 7, 1979.

[10]*Living, Learning, and Caring,* Ginn and Company, 1981, p. 17.

[11]Texas Textbook Adoption Changes and Corrections Requested of Publishers, 1982, p. 36.

[12]*Living, Learning, and Caring,* p. 20.

[13]Texas Textbook Adoption Changes and Corrections Requested of Publishers, 1982, p. 37.

[14]Presentation on "Families with Children," National Research Forum on Family Issues, April 10, 1980, cited by McGraw, *The Family, Feminism, and the Therapeutic State,* p. 20.

[15]Public Law 95-561—November 1, 1978, Education Amendments of 1978, 20 USC 2701, "Protection of Pupil Rights," SEC. 1250. Section 439 (b), 20 USC 1232h.

[16]*Wisconsin v. Yoder,* 1972 (406 U.S. 205, 232): "The primary role of the parents in the upbringing of their children is now established beyond debate as an enduring American tradition." *Prince v. Massachusetts* (321 U.S. 158, 166): "It is cardinal with us that the custody, care, and nurture of the child reside first in the parents, whose primary function and freedom include preparation for obligations the state can neither supply nor hinder."

[17]S. Robert Lichter and Stanley Rothman, *Public Opinion* magazine, cited by the *St. Louis Globe Democrat,* December 31, 1981.

[18]*The Connecticut Mutual Life Report on American Values in the '80s: The Impact of Belief,* Connecticut Mutual Life Insurance Co., Hartford, Connecticut, 1981.

[19]*Vital Signs: Emerging Social Trends and the Future of American Christianity*, Crossway Books, 1984, pp. 4-5.
[20]Cited by McGraw, *The Family, Feminism, and the Therapeutic State*, p. 23.
[21]Judith S. Wallerstein and Joan B. Kelly, "Children and Divorce: A Review," *Social Work*, November 1979, pp. 468-475, cited by McGraw, *The Family, Feminism, and the Therapeutic State*, p. 24.
[22]*Homemaking Skills for Everyday Living*, Goodheart/Willcox, 1981, p. 87.
[23]*Ibid.*, p. 88.
[24]*Ibid.*, p. 102.
[25]"Guidelines For Creating Positive Sexual and Racial Images in Educational Materials," Macmillan Publishing Company, cited in Nicholas von Hoffman, "Heading for Doublethink, Literally," *The Washington Post*, July 21, 1975.
[26]*Ibid.*
[27]*Ibid.*
[28]"Examples of 2,274 Changes Requested of Publishers in 1975 Texas Textbook Adoptions," as cited in Educational Research Analysts, Forms T-441 and T-442.
[29]*Married Life*, Chas. A. Bennett Co., Inc., 1976, p. 37.
[30]Mel and Norma Gabler to Texas Commissioner of Education and Texas State Textbook Committee, 8/11/81, Austin, Texas.
[31]Verified by numerous national surveys including: Gallup, *Better Homes and Gardens*, and Connecticut Mutual Life Insurance Company.
[32]Isaiah 5:20, KJV.

HOW TO GET BETTER BOOKS INTO YOUR SCHOOL AND SURVIVE

The more he read, the angrier Jeff, a husky ex-sailor, became. When he finished reading the book his fifteen-year-old daughter had brought home from school, he was boiling. "I'm gonna go see that principal and put him straight," he told his wife. By the time he parked at the school, he had a plan.

A secretary ushered Jeff into the principal's office. Once introductions were over, he began telling a bawdy story while the school official sat fidgeting. Jeff kept on, throwing in obscenities, profanities, and explicit sexual descriptions.

Finally, he stopped. "Does the language I'm using make you uncomfortable?" Jeff asked.

"Well, yes," the principal replied. "I'm not used to hearing such talk in my office. Could we get on with the reason you came to see me?"

"It bothers me too," Jeff said, as he pulled his daughter's book from his coat pocket. Every offensive word I've spoken came from this book—which was assigned to *my* daughter by *this* school! I want the book removed."

The principal immediately became apologetic. "Yes, yes, of course. I didn't know all that was in there. I'll talk to the teacher right away. We'll do something about that book."

Jeff stood up and leaned over the desk. "Maybe I can help you a little." He ripped the book in half, threw the pieces into the wastebasket, and stalked out.

While we don't recommend Jeff's method for dealing with offensive books, we *do* admire his courage. Actually, it's far better to deal with offensive textbooks *before* the school purchases them. Once in the classroom, it's virtually impossible to get a bad book out. School officials will ask you to fill out a long form, listing in detail what you don't like. They'll defend their decision to buy the book. They'll hassle you with arguments. They'll plead budgetary restraints. They'll wear you down with meetings and consultations. Only if the book gets a lot of bad publicity will they be likely to act. Even then, you'll be regarded as a troublemaker and your child may suffer. All this just to get rid of one bad book!

Preventing offensive textbooks from getting into your child's school will take time and preparation; but in the long run, you'll experience fewer frustrations and accomplish far more than if you try to deal with the problem *after* the fact.

Know Your Rights

Before you begin your efforts, an awareness of a few important facts is crucial. One, you have rights as a parent which the school must respect. Two, in standing up for traditional values and the teaching of knowledge and skills, you'll be representing the majority view of parents and students across the country. Don't let educators convince you otherwise.

Here are six legal rights which all parents have in regard to their child's education:

(1) *The Federal Protection of Pupil Rights Act.*[1] Enacted into federal law in 1978, this legislation *forbids* schools to (1) subject students to psychological examination or treatment, (2) require students to reveal "political affiliations," "sexual behavior and attitudes," "mental and psychological problems potentially embarrassing to the student or his family," or (3) ask students for "critical appraisals" of behavior and attitudes of family members without the "prior written consent of the parent." This act is popularly known as the Hatch Amendment.

The U.S. Department of Education didn't get around to holding hearings on this law until 1984.[2] Here are a few of the shocking incidents reported during these hearings: A woman testified that she had two abortions in high school—and was held up to fellow students as a role model of "responsible" sexual activity. A mother reported her son committed suicide after taking courses that reinforced his negative attitudes and depression. Another parent told how her son was traumatized when assigned to write a graphic description of the death of his pet dog. Still other parents cited sex-ed assignments which required explicit, nonjudgmental discussions of every kind of sex act.

You can imagine the howl that arose against the Hatch Amendment from humanistic educators. The NEA newsletter, *NEA Now,* called the proposed regulations "chilling challenges to academic freedom" which will "open the floodgates for classroom meddling by right-wing political groups."[3] (The NEA and other educational elitists have moved so far to the left that anyone who retains a sense of balance is to their right.)

If your school pleads ignorance of the Protection of Pupil Rights Act, obtain a copy from your U.S. Representative or Senators, and then confront school officials to get action.

(2) *State laws that protect parental rights.* Oklahoma has a Parents' Consent Law requiring that all instructional material used with a "program designed to explore or develop new or unproven teaching methods or techniques" be made available for inspection by parents or guardians of students in the program. Such programs may be violating juvenile codes, criminal codes, and/or child abuse laws. It further requires parental consent for psychological or psychiatric probing of students' views on sexual behavior and attitudes, critical appraisals of family members, and religious beliefs. A number of Oklahoma parents have used this law to stop "values clarification" in their schools. Check to see if your state has a similar law.

(3) *State or district guidelines for textbooks.* Oklahoma, Texas, and a number of other jurisdictions have set standards which textbooks must meet. These generally require curriculums to be objective in content, not to encourage civil disorder or disrespect for the law, teach high moral standards and obedience to law, foster the work ethic, teach the positive principles and benefits of free enterprise, and emphasize the importance of traditional family roles. Many school officials are not aware of, or choose to ignore, these rules in making textbook selections. Parents often must call these guidelines to the attention of textbook adoption/selection committees.

(4) *The "Establishment" Clause of the First Amendment to the U.S. Constitution.* Judge Braswell Deen, Jr., Chief Judge of the Court of Appeals of Georgia says,

This Constitutional right of students and parents is being violated [in education] by . . . forcing on students humanistic, non-theistic origins and values to the exclusion of theistic origins and absolute values.[4] You have a right to resist such intrusions.

(5) *The "Free Exercise" Clause of the First Amendment.* This right is violated when evolution, situation ethics, and other humanistic doctrines are foisted on students by subtle coercion, indoctrination, or peer pressure from other indoctrinated students.

(6) *The "Equal Protection" Clause of the Fourteenth Amendment.* "Equal protection" is a part of the civil rights guaranteed theists. Humanists have no right to force their religious views on students under the guise of "neutral" education.

Over three fourths of Americans prefer traditional morality.[5] Educators will admit this. "If a referendum were taken today," says Mario Fantini, dean of education at a branch of the State University of New York, "there's no doubt in my mind that 70 percent of the parents would opt for the old-fashioned kinds of education they had themselves, and only 30 percent for the innovations."[6]

Where do the kids stand? A Gallup Poll youth survey showed 80 percent "would welcome more emphasis on traditional family ties," 72 percent "wouldn't welcome more acceptance of marijuana usage," and 69 percent "wouldn't welcome less emphasis on working hard." Students making better grades were more likely than others to endorse traditional values.[7]

You're Not Alone

Do all school personnel accept the doctrines of "progressive" education? Certainly not. But peer and job pressures keep many from speaking out. Numerous teachers have told us privately, "I agree with you almost 100 percent. But don't ever mention my name."

> Some teachers and administrators who hold more traditional values than the NEA have formed their own professional organizations. In addition, two Christian teachers' organizations offer support and fellowship for individuals in this field.[8]

School board members are much like teachers. Many agree with us as individuals. But get them together at a public meeting and they'll almost invariably defend the professionals they have hired. We've never met a board member who read a textbook—unless a parent had challenged him to or a protest movement was under way. Many are bamboozled by school administrators (who haven't read the books, either) to believe that any parent who objects to a textbook is a troublemaker.

The law and a majority of Americans are on the side of those who want better textbooks. The educational elitists are against this majority and will fight them all the way. We saw this happen the first time we filed a petition against a book. Nothing has happened since to change our minds. If you're determined to join the fight, know from the outset that you'll have a hard row to hoe. But you *can* survive and win! What can you do?

Build a parents' group for strength and concerted action. Though you shouldn't depend solely on the PTA for help, you can gain clout by being involved with this organization.

Recruit friends individually. Show them marked copies of objectionable portions in actual textbooks.

Write your state education office for information on how textbooks are adopted. Ask how parents can be involved. Request the rules of procedure.

Publishers offering books for approval should be required to make books available to the public. In Texas, they are placed in regional educational libraries. Some publishers will even sell you books at the price they charge schools. Be courteous, but firm. Get the books for review before the local textbook adoption committee meets.

Be selective in what you review. Take one subject area of particular concern one year, such as social studies, then examine literature the next, and history the next. Or assign various subjects or subtopics to review among members of your group.

We already have reviews for many books.[9] These can save you countless hours of painstaking examination, but use our reviews only as a starter. Read the books closely yourself. Look at the headings, subheads, and illustrations. Ponder the methodology. Blatantly offensive material will jump out at you. It's more important for you to grasp the humanistic and immoral philosophies that are being *subtly* promoted. Look to see how information is balanced, pro and con, on controversial issues.

We examine textbooks for content which stresses problems, but few solutions; emphasizes America's failings, rather than achievements; condones immorality and ignores morality; attacks religion and Christianity, but gives no suggestion of their benefits; belittles biblical statements or treats them as myths; teaches the occult, but does not warn of its dangers; presents evidence for evolution as though it were established fact, but censors empirically tested scientific evidence against evolution; destroys confidence in traditional values; slights parents and their teachings; constantly emphasizes change without absolutes or fixed values; and stresses realism, but only from a negative view.

Forewarned Is Forearmed

We've already said the battle will not be easy. But most of the hassles you'll get from the education establishment are predictable. Here are some of the statements you'll hear most often, followed by ways you can counter them.

"Teachers have rights too, the most basic of which is academic freedom."

This works two ways. What about the student's right *not* to be taught from unacceptable texts? Where is the student's right *not* to read offensive material? The teacher merely acts in place of the parent. His or her right is subservient to the parent's rights and responsibilities for the child.[10]

"Why are you meddling? Leave the selection of textbooks to the school."

Are only educators permitted access to the democratic process in education? Parents decide what their children read and see in the home. Where is the law that says this right ends when their children pass through the school door?

"But if you needed surgery, you wouldn't operate on yourself. You'd go to a trained surgeon. Why not let the professional educators do what they're trained to do?"

A surgeon is only as good as his instruments and equipment. Would you go to one who used dirty, unsterilized, or ineffective instruments? Why should I permit my children's minds to be subjected to instruments of education—textbooks—which I believe will harm them?

While we're dealing with the claim that "professionals know best," we might question their track record. Why have the "professionals" fostered such turkeys as "new math," "new English," "look-say" reading, and open classrooms? Why has discipline become so bad that policemen must patrol the halls of many schools? Why has there been a steady decrease in vocabulary and college entrance examination grades? Why has illiteracy, crime, VD, sexual promiscuity, and drug use risen so high?

We were taught that if you plant potatoes, you get potatoes. If you plant rebellion and immorality in children's minds by teaching them that only they can decide what is right and wrong, that parents are old-fashioned, and that the Judeo-Christian Bible is a book of fairy tales, then what can you expect? Garbage in—garbage out!

"So, you think you have a corner on the market of justice, truth, right, and beauty?"

No. I simply believe that America was founded on Judeo-Christian values and I want my children to be taught this heritage. The great majority of parents desire this orientation, not the garbage of situation ethics, "values clarification," and destructive political ideologies.

"You're trying to interfere with a child's right to choose his own values."

Children in the lower grades are much too young to be asked to decide whether stealing, for example, is right or wrong for them. The school's duty is to transmit the moral values held by the majority of Americans. Textbooks treat the children as primitives, as if Western civilization has nothing to offer.

The truth is that the child does not really choose his own values in school. Rather, he's brainwashed to believe that there are no absolute values. He's also taught that a group consensus should determine what is right and wrong. When a child is asked to decide, say, whether sexual intercourse before marriage is right or wrong, textbooks and peer pressure usually come down on the wrong side. I have a right to interfere when my child is being influenced in these ways.

"Why do you object to research questions on subjects such as the Great Depression, Watergate, Communism, sexual mores, etc.?"

I don't, provided the curriculum and the teachers provide sufficient information. What I object to is students being given inadequate history and other information which will distort their education. If the books can't be objective on controversial matters, then they shouldn't raise them at all.

"You're asking for censorship and trying to impose your views on what the children of other parents are taught."

The humanistic education establishment imposed its views on the majority of parents long before we raised our voices. Text books have been censored of morality, patriotism, and free enterprise for years. Why is it called censorship when parents seek to disclose textbook content? Why must children, in a school supported by my taxes, be forced to study content which does not give equal time to their parents' views on important subjects? Why must they read and think about some material which is too offensive to be put in newspapers or spoken over radio and TV?

"Why are you objecting to negativism in school books? Don't you realize that a child has to live in the real world?"

Are pornography, obscenity, and violence a part of most persons' "real" world? Are crime, violence, cruelty, and suicide the daily fare of the majority? Since when is a small segment of society the "real" world? My friends do not use obscene language, or at least not in public, before children. It is not representative of my community and associates and it should not be portrayed as the norm for students.

"But these books you object to are judged to be of excellent literary quality."

Literary quality is in the eye of the beholder. Why can't you include stories that magnify friendship and compassion? Why dwell on the worst in humanity?

"Why do you object to classics like 'Jack and the Beanstalk'?"

I don't. It's the way they're handled, with the implication given in follow-up discussions that it's sometimes right to steal or do other wrong things.

"The Bible includes accounts of murder and immorality. Why do you condemn textbooks for doing the same?"

That's a sorry defense which tells a lot about the ignorance of some educators. The Bible explains what is right and wrong and shows judgment and punishment. The textbooks do not.

"Why are you stirring up controversy?"

I am not the point of controversy; textbooks are. Some parents like the philosophies taught in the curriculum, but the majority of us who believe in traditional values do not.

"You're a part of a national network of extremists trying to take over the schools."

No national organization connects individuals and groups who protest against undesirable curriculum material. Yet a very obvious network exists in socialistic, "progressive" education which promotes humanistic, immoral, anti-religious propaganda. This network is held together by job and peer pressures in publishing houses, teacher colleges, state and federal education departments, and local educational circles. Would a teacher or principal ever get a promotion if he or she took a strong stand against the Humanism that is taught in textbooks?

Effective Strategies

From our years of experience and learning from others, here are some hints which, if followed, will keep you sane and on your feet in the battle for better books in the classroom:

(1) *Try to get influential individuals on your side before you attend any public meeting.* Without referring to the book over which you're concerned, ask newspaper editors, clergymen, or elected officials whether they agree or disagree with such propositions as: "Do you think second-graders should decide for themselves whether and when it's right or wrong to steal? Do you believe students should be taught the advantages of the free enterprise system?" After they've agreed or disagreed, show them the position the book takes. If they too feel that the book takes an inappropriate stand on the issue, ask them if they would be willing to testify to that effect at a textbook adoption hearing. Community leaders carry influence; it helps to have them on your side.

(2) *Prepare and know ahead of time what you will say.* At one time, we were allowed to take twelve minutes to present our objections to a book at the state hearings. Now, we have only six minutes in which to cover one book or a series. Consequently, Norma types her speech out, times herself, and practically knows it by memory before she ever gets up to speak.

(3) *Simplify the semantics.* Understand such terms as values clarification, social orientation, ethical relativism, etc. If educators use these terms, ask them to stop and define such "educationese" for the sake of the uninitiated.

(4) *Stick to issues. Avoid personalities.* Do not name authors, and mention publishers only when necessary. Deal strictly with content and avoid loaded terms like "Communist," "left-winger," and "pervert" when you must cite personalities.

(5) *Always leave your opponent an "out."* Give nim the opportunity to say that he doesn't agree with the book, but is only following orders. This allows him to "save face" and may win him to your side.

(6) *Hold some of your best points in reserve.* Having a good comeback will show a committee or an audience that you really

know the issues.

(7) *Keep your cool.* When opponents resort to invectives, keep your head high, your face smiling, and your voice low, but loud enough to be clearly understood.

(8) *Stay on the offensive.* Your political and religious beliefs are not on trial. Offensive textbooks are. Ignore irrelevant charges. Say, "My personal opinions and yours are not the subject of this discussion. We're talking about school curriculum." Then get on with your objections.

(9) *Hold the book defender's feet to the fire.* If an opponent hassles you, ask, "Have you read the book(s)?" If he hasn't or has scanned only a portion, state: "You're supporting something you know nothing or little about, while I have examined the book in detail." If he persists in defending the book, say, "Evidently, you are an employee of the school system and are obligated to defend the curriculum."

(10) *Use the media.* Approach your local media on the assumption that they will want to report fairly the positions of all sides. If a reporter displays bias or is curt, patiently explain that you and your group have rights as parents and are only working for better books. Show him or her some of the offensive material in books and/or provide copies of quotes. Do this matter-of-factly without lecturing or making accusations.

Prepare a professionally typed press release for each major announcement or event relating to your group's activities on the textbook front. If you or your group don't know how to prepare a press release, get a book on public relations from the library, or ask a friend in the media. These releases should run a maximum of two pages and always include the name, address, and phone number of one or more contact persons in your group.

Write letters to the editor, no longer than 300 words, stating problems and citing quotes from objectionable textbooks. Avoid generalities and diatribes. Encourage members of your group to write for publication in local papers.

If your group or cause is criticized in an editorial, ask for the privilege of replying. Most newspapers will accept an "op-ed" piece that's well written and to the point.

Make and distribute to your group a list of the call-in radio talk shows heard in your area. Encourage members to call and cite specific problems in curriculum. Again, deal with specifics, not generalities: "Why must my children be required to study the Communist party structure before their own nation's political parties in an American government textbook?"[11] is much better than, "Why must my children be indoctrinated in Communism in school?" "Why must my children be taught that under some circumstances it is wrong *not* to lie?"[12] is preferable to a tirade about how textbooks are attacking traditional values. Always have the name and pages of the books at hand to back up your complaints.

Your group's activities may provoke an editorial on a local TV station. Ask for time to give a rebuttal. School board member Alice Moore, who supported the parents in Charleston, West Virginia, got the crusade rolling against bad books in her school system by taking advantage of such an opportunity.

Never attempt to read profanities or obscenities over the air. "Bleep, bleep, bleep" is more dramatic. If you're at a public meeting or in a studio, ask the host or moderator to read the bleeps. He probably won't, but you will have made your point.

(11) *Persist and persevere.* Textbooks didn't become instruments of social change and Humanist propaganda overnight. It will take time to change them. Hang in there. Learn from your bloopers. When knocked down, get up and get back in the fight. You've learned what *not* to do next time.

And don't despair if you stand alone or your group is small. Remember:

- One vote gave America the English language instead of German.
- Thomas Jefferson and John Quincy Adams were elected President by one vote in the Electoral College.
- One vote gave Rutherford Hayes the presidency of the United States, and this vote was cast by a Congressman from Indiana who had himself won his own election by only one vote.
- One vote changed France from a monarchy to a republic.
- One vote gave Adolph Hitler leadership of the Nazi party.
- One vote per precinct elected John Kennedy President of the United States.

Never underestimate the power of *one*.[13]

To remind us constantly of this fact, we pasted this quotation in our den:

I am only one,
But I am one.
I cannot do everything,
But I can do something.
And because I cannot do everything,
I will not refuse to do the some-
   thing that I can do.
                —*Edward Everett Hale*

Footnotes

[1] Public Law 95-561—Nov. 1, 1978, Education Amendments of 1978, 20 USC 2701, "Protection of Pupil Rights," SEC 1250. Section 439(b) 20 USC 1232h.

[2] We urge you to read a transcript of the shocking testimony at these hearings in *Child Abuse in the Classroom*, Phyllis Schlafly, ed., $4.95, Pere Marquette Press, Alton, IL 62002. See Chapter 8 for excerpts from this book.

[3] *NEA Now*, April 16, 1984, p. 1. This newsletter also bemoaned the opening of teacher's files, "Enforced as currently written . . . 'child privacy' regulations would mandate that *all* instructional material—including teachers' manuals, films, and tapes—must be made available for parental inspection. . . . The regulations would make such basic services and courses as student counseling, grade-level testing, drug prevention programs, and sex education immediately vulnerable to attacks from anti-public school ideologues."

[4] Judge Braswell Deen states there are five laws many schools are violating. These include the "Establishment" Clause and the "Free Exercise" Clause of the First Amendment; the "Equal Protection" Clause of the Fourteenth Amendment; the Hatch Amendment; and state laws against child abuse, both physical and mental.

[5] Substantiated by surveys including: Gallup, *Better Homes and Gardens*, Connecticut Mutual Life Insurance Co.

[6] *Newsweek*, October 31, 1974, p. 87.

[7] *Houston Post*, "Gallup Poll/youth survey. Teens endorse traditional social values," November 28, 1979.

[8] National Association of Christian Educators (NACE), Dr. Robert Simonds, President, 3125 Van Buren, P.O. Box 3200, Costa Mesa, CA 92626; Christian Educators Association (CEA), 1410 W. Colorado Blvd., Pasadena, CA 91105.

[9]Available from The Gablers, P.O. Box 7518, Longview, TX 75607. See Appendix 2 for ordering information.
[10]Numerous Supreme Court rulings uphold parental rights. For example: *Abington v. Schempp*, 374 U.S. 203-320 (1963); *Pierce v. Society of Sisters*, 268 U.S. 510, 535 (1924); *Mercer v. Michigan*, 1974, as cited in vol. 43 Law Weekly, p. 3354.
[11]*United States Government: The People Decide*, Science Research Associates, Inc., 1979, p. 99, Teacher's Manual, pp. 27-28.
[12]*Inquiries in Sociology*, Allyn and Bacon, 1978, p. 45.
[13]"I'm Only One; What Can I Do?" Stedman Corporation, Asheboro, North Carolina 27203, back cover.

WHAT MORE CAN PARENTS DO?

President Truman kept a sign on his desk that declared, "The Buck Stops Here." Parents should put a similar notice in their home: "The Buck *Begins* and Stops Here." Parents are first and foremost responsible for their child's education. God said to parents—not the state—"Train up a child in the way he should go."[1]

In fact, when the Hebrews were enroute from Egypt to the Promised Land, God instructed parents:

> And these words, which I command thee this day, shall be in thine heart: And thou shalt teach them diligently unto thy children, and shalt talk of them when thou sittest in thine house, and when thou walkest by the way, and when thou liest down, and when thou risest up.[2]

The American pioneers adopted this very pattern. Like the Jews, they saw the family as the primary source of education. Parents introduced children to the Bible, language, social customs, values, and vocational skills. It was their duty to prepare offspring for entry into society. Then, as the nation grew, community schools were set up to aid parents.

We documented in chapter 2 how government—first state, then federal—began taking over more and more educational responsibilities until schools and textbooks became the mess they are today. Thankfully, the pendulum is beginning to swing back. Thousands of parents are recognizing that they, not the school or some government agency, are primarily responsible for their children. As a Colorado couple told us in a letter:

> Because of our deeply held biblical convictions concerning our children's education and our responsibility as parents relating thereto, we cannot delegate that responsibility to the public school system.

Too many parents, when a child is ready for kindergarten or first grade, say to the school, "You educate him." Parents attend a couple of PTA meetings, patronize the school fair, and occasionally help their child with homework—and think they've done their duty. Then when the kid starts bad-mouthing them and develops other bad habits, they blame everybody but themselves.

Professor Herbert Walberg of the University of Illinois says research shows that schools cannot be effective without the participation of the child's family.[3] Melvin Schneider, professor emeritus of the University of Northern Iowa at Cedar Rapids, states that "parents are the most important determinant of how children learn and how they behave."[4] But the "parent participation" which public educators rate so highly requires parents to go along with whatever the school teaches.

A growing number of informed parents are deciding they *cannot* go along when the school undermines parental authority and drives a wedge between them and their child. These are the very parents who take their responsibilities most seriously. They want their child to advance in skills and knowledge while remaining loyal to home values. What are they to do when they see the school is failing their child?

What Parents Can Do

Most wise parents recognize the shortcomings and limitations of public schools long before their children register there. We get frequent calls from such mothers and fathers, asking, "How can I prepare my child to cope with what he'll face in school? What can I do to supplement inadequate teaching? How can I teach him real values?"

First, start by finding out if the school teaches genuine phonics. If not, start teaching him to read by sounding out letters and blends of letters—before the school gives him "look-say" or some form of phony phonics. Then work with him regularly after he enters school. Reading is basic to all other skills. (See our *Handbook 9*, "Phonics," which includes listings of suitable curriculums for teaching true phonics.)[5]

Second, set a moral example for him. Let him see that you tell the truth and obey the law. Take him to Sunday School. Have family discussions about Bible lessons. Pray with him daily. Teach him to know and love God. Keep communication lines open, so that you'll know when the school is challenging your values. And, as we stressed in the previous chapter, join the fight for better textbooks.

Third, there might even be a more suitable alternative public school in your area. "Basic" or "fundamental" public schools give more attention to skills, homework, and achievement. They generally have honor rolls, dress codes, and strong discipline. A list of such schools is available from the Council for Basic Education, 725 Fifteenth Street, N.W., Washington, D.C. 20005.

If there is an alternative school in your city, it will likely have a waiting list. Though it probably will not teach traditional morality, it will spend less time than regular schools on "values clarification" and other destructive methodologies.

The Private School Option

A good private school may be even more available, but you must consider the cost of tuition, transportation, and the purchase of materials.

A *Newsweek* poll found that 54 percent of parents with children in public schools have considered the private alternative, and 23 percent would likely switch to private schools if Congress approved tuition tax credits of $250 to $500 a year. Private school enrollment increased 19 percent in the 1970s while public school enrollment dropped, especially in the West.[6]

You'll hear much self-serving propaganda from public school educators who oppose and fear the private school movement. They claim many private schools were begun to beat integration. Some *were* started for that purpose during the racial conflicts of the 1960s, but the *Newsweek* study says "few" clear signs of racial prejudice now exist. In fact, black and Hispanic parents, in large numbers, are opting for private schools. Children of these two minorities now make up one sixth of the total enrollment of Catholic parochial schools.[7]

It cannot be denied that children in private schools score

178

higher on standardized tests than those in public education. Public school people say this is because private institutions attract better students and receive stronger parental support. However, research shows that the very students who do worst in public schools show marked improvement after entering private schools.[8]

Public school promoters also carp that if they had more money they could do better. But the private schools do far better on much less. St. Michael's, a fine Catholic school in Los Angeles, with a student body that's 75 percent black and 17 percent Hispanic, spends only $441 per student each year—compared to $3,000 expended per pupil in the California public system. Private school teachers' salaries are lower, but even if they were tripled, private education still would cost much less per child.

The most expensive private schools are the "prep" academies which have high scholastic requirements and strict discipline, but may not take a stand for traditional morality. Student tuition may be as high as $5,000-$6,000 a year.[9]

The Christian School Boom

European immigrants started Catholic schools in the nineteenth century because they considered American public schools too Protestant (nobody makes that accusation anymore!). In 1956, Catholics enrolled almost 87 percent of all students attending private schools. By 1979, that total was down to 67 percent.[10]

The basic reason for this change in percentages is the boom in fundamentalist-Christian schools. We estimate that at least 10,000 such schools are now in operation, with three new ones added every day. Families are leaving the public system because of the very problems we've documented in preceding chapters. A biology professor at a Christian college testifies to this decline:

> Fifteen years ago my wife and I registered our two oldest children in public schools. With a lot of help from us, they survived. Now we're sending our youngest child to a private Christian school because public education has worsened.

We want the public schools reformed. Our fight for better textbooks proves that interest. Meanwhile, we can understand why parents who believe in traditional values would want to have their children learn skills and be taught real morality.

We work with parents of many faiths. Catholic and Jewish schools have long been established. Because the fundamentalist-Christian movement is so new, these schools are very diverse in facilities, faculties, academic standards, and financial resources.

They also differ on how they deal with government agencies. None disagree with the need to comply with health, fire, and safety regulations, and some accept state-mandated teacher certification and programs. But others balk at this point and refuse to submit to any licensing or state accreditation. They see their school as an extension of religious faith and practice, protected from state interference by the First Amendment.

Get full information about any school before enrolling your child. Good Christian schools will have Bible classes, compulsory chapel, and dress codes. Talk to parents and children already in the school. Is it meeting their needs?

How Good Are Christian Schools?

How do Christian school students' test scores stack up against national averages? According to a 1983 study by the Association of Christian Schools International—which requires that member schools meet certain academic standards[11]—students in ACSI schools scored significantly higher on a standardized achievement test than students in public schools at all grade levels.[12] Eleventh-graders ranked sixteen months higher in terms of achievement than the national average.

Many Christian schools also follow the Accelerated Christian Education (ACE) system. ACE focuses on individualized instruction, academic achievement, and integration of Bible learning with skill disciplines. Each student has his own "office"—a chair or desk partitioned from other students. The curriculum is comprised of Packets of Accelerated Christian Education (PACES), which are twenty-five to thirty-five page booklets on English, math, science, social studies, and the Bible. Tests appear throughout the booklets and students must check themselves on comprehension as they move along. When a student completes a book, he is tested by the teacher on all the material and must score at least 80 percent to advance to the next packet on that subject.

ACE curriculum is modeled after Bible-saturated textbooks used in the community schools of early America. A math problem, for example, might require the student to add up members of the twelve tribes of Israel and find the average number in a tribe. A sentence to be diagramed might describe a Bible character.[13] This practice also is used by some other Christian publishers.

ACE has been very effective for starting small Christian schools. It is local-church oriented and not available for individuals. The second edition of ACE curriculum has been edited of sectarian doctrine to make it suitable for schools of all persuasions, and is available to individuals in book form as the "Basic Education" curriculum. Alpha Omega Publications of Tempe, Arizona produces a program similar to the ACE second edition. Traditional curriculum materials, using textbooks, are available from several Christian publishers. By far, the largest publisher of Christian textbooks is A BEKA Publishers of Pensacola, Florida.

We recommend curriculums in our *Handbook 6* which includes a long list of worthy textbooks, both religious and secular. This list is constantly being revised. Our *Handbook 27* provides listings of reputable reading and literature books.[14]

We urge you to check the curriculum used by the private school in which you are considering enrolling your child; probably over half the textbooks used in Christian schools actually are humanistic texts. The most dangerous texts usually are not the ones with blatant content, but those in which the humanism is so subtly woven in that it is not easily discernible. We were at a Christian schools conference when the executive director of a church-related school association began examining the marked and indexed textbooks we had on display. Visibly agitated, he held up a book and declared, "This text is used in our school. When I get home some heads are going to roll!"

Another question to consider: Are faculty members, and perhaps parents also, required to sign a statement of faith? If so, are you comfortable with the beliefs? Looking to the other side, do any of the teachers accept evolution, situation ethics, or other doctrines of Humanism?

Take everything into consideration. Choose the best possible school for your child.

What About Home Schooling?

What if you can't stomach what the public school is teaching, but are unable to send your child to a suitable private school?

Home schooling, which Christian psychologist James Dobson calls "the wave of the future,"[15] might be a possibility. Estimates of the number of children already studying at home range from 10,000 to 1 million.[16]

Why is the range of estimates so wide? Many parents are teaching children "under cover" without notifying any school or government agency. Some take advantage of laws allowing late enrollment. In thirty-three states and the District of Columbia, children do not have to enroll until age seven; in Arizona, Pennsylvania, Washington State, and Puerto Rico, entrance is not required until age eight.[17] Furthermore, some states, including Texas, do not have a definitive legal ruling on home schools. The Texas Education Agency doesn't know how many home schools exist because only local courts can decide when truancy laws are violated.

Legal confusion pervades many states about home schooling which occurs after the required age of registration. Circuit Court judges in two Tennessee counties ruled in 1984 that the state's attendance law is too vague and parents opting for home schooling cannot be prosecuted. Tennessee's law is practically identical to statutes in fourteen other states where courts have not as yet ruled on mandatory attendance in public or private schools.[18] Unless the Tennessee legislature enacts a barrier, parents in that state may have clear sailing ahead.

Eventually, the constitutionality of home schools may go to the U.S. Supreme Court; there, the question could be settled for all states. In 1925 the Supreme Court struck down a state law against private education on grounds that the act "interferes with the liberty of parents and guardians to direct the upbringing and education of children.[19] In 1972 the High Court ruled that:

> The primary role of the parents in the upbringing of their children is now established beyond debate as an enduring American tradition.[20]

How Helpful Is Home Schooling?

Dr. Raymond Moore is a developmental psychologist whose research on the family and school has appeared in virtually every educational journal in the U.S. and abroad. In their helpful book, *Home Grown Kids*, Dr. Moore and his wife Dorothy "do not know of one such home school in the nation [from hundreds of cases in their files] in which the students are not performing well above average academically and behaviorally. And socially they generally excel."[21]

The Moores tell of a confrontation between parent Douglas Ort and the state of New York, in which Ort was ordered to put his children in public school. When Ort asked what law he'd be violating if he refused, a state officer said, "criminal child neglect."

"Our children are not neglected," Ort insisted.

"I didn't make the laws," the man apologized, "but I must follow instructions. . . . We must make sure they are up to state standards."

"What standards do you have in mind?"

"Any good standardized test, such as—"

"What is the toughest of all?"

"The Stanford Achievement battery is a good one."

"Then please test them," the father politely challenged.

Thirteen children from six home schools were tested. All achieved scores in the upper 10 percent of the national average. One of Doug Ort's two children scored in the top 4 percent and the other tied with a neighbor's child in the top 1 percent.[22]

The widely publicized testing cooled the ardor of some overzealous educators in New York. But the pressure is still on in many communities in other states.

"History has never uncovered a better educational system than the warm one-on-one response of a concerned parent to his child," says Dr. Moore. He notes that five top leaders during the Second World War—Franklin Roosevelt, Winston Churchill, Konrad Adenauer, Douglas MacArthur, and George Patton—were all home-schooled. Writers Agatha Christie and Pearl Buck, and Supreme Court Justice Sandra O'Conner, also were taught by their parents.[23]

According to Dr. Moore, many child development authorities "now acknowledge that quality of learning depends upon the maturity of the learner. . . . For most children, including the brightest, this maturity seldom comes before ages eight to twelve." He cites University of Chicago researcher Benjamin Bloom, once a booster of the "Head Start" program, who now admits that parents are the best teachers.[24]

Perhaps the most frequent criticism of home schooling is that it will stunt students' social development. Studies done at the University of North Carolina and Stanford and Cornell Universities indicate otherwise. Cornell's Urie Bronfenbrenner reports that until the fifth or sixth grade, children who spend more of their free time with their peers than with their parents will become peer dependent. To the extent that they are pressured by peer values, they will fail in self-worth, optimism, and respect for parents.[25] Thus it is easy to understand why children with more parental socialization than peer socialization until age twelve seldom are involved in crime, violence, or other immoral acts.

Thinking of Home Schooling?

Home schooling, especially for young children, has many advantages. But before you embark, count the cost. Our *Handbooks 12-A* and *12-B*[26] contain a wealth of basic information, including the addresses for several home schooling organizations. Helpful books are available in many bookstores. To give you an idea of what is involved, here are several relevant suggestions for would-be home teachers:

(1) Discuss thoroughly the pluses and minuses of the program with your whole family. Your family must be absolutely sold on it and each member must accept his or her responsibilities.

(2) Start collecting materials you will need, including desks, books, chalkboard, and other necessities. A list of resources is given in our *Handbook 12-A*, cited above.

(3) Start teaching your child early. The Moores, in *Home Grown Kids*, give directions from birth on. Obviously, more formalized and structured teaching will not come until later.

(4) When you are ready to begin a formal teaching program, develop a structure and schedule. Follow a well-rounded curriculum. Assign homework. Give tests. Provide everything that your child might be expected to receive in a school with his peers.

Our friend Ginny Baker was a pioneer in the home schooling movement and is the author of *Teaching Your Children at Home*.[27] She laid down the law with her four children from the beginning: "Starting at nine in the morning, I'm your teacher. We're going to follow the strict rules in our school that we have in our home." A few weeks of this practice, away from public schools, resulted in a remarkable improvement in her children's attitudes and discipline problems faded away.

Her son, Chris, (home-taught during grades six through

twelve) has just graduated from prestigious Texas A & M University with a degree in biomedical science and will be applying to both veterinary and medical schools. Since science was Ginny's *weakest* point, this bears out the truth that a parent need not be a master in every subject. He or she needs only to provide motivation and resources for the student to learn.

(5) Link up with other parent-teachers for fellowship and sharing of knowledge, experiences, and resources. In Chattanooga, some thirty-five parents have formed the "Greentree School." Each family pays a fee of $120 per year which contributes to the salary of a part-time "headmaster" who also teaches in the education department of a Christian college. A family can enroll children, receive training on teaching methods, get assistance in locating good curriculum, participate in standardized testing, and share in extracurricular activities.[28] Parents who use the Christian Liberty curricululm[29] become satellite affiliates of that academy.

(6) Bone up on state educational laws. Michael Farris, founder of the Home School Legal Defense Association, advises:

> The best defense against state harassment is to be prepared ahead of time with a legal plan and a well-documented set of records that will show your child's educational progress.[30]

Know Your Rights

The Bible gives parents complete responsibility and control over their children's education. The U.S. Supreme Court has consistently acknowledged parents' rights to control their children's education, provided they do not neglect it.[31] Despite this fact, humanistic educators typically claim that school-age children are wards of the state, and that parents have no rights over their children's education. Apparently many lawyers, overzealous district attorneys, and some lower courts are unaware of the preponderance of law in the parents' favor.

Do not let their ignorance or arrogance intimidate you, as you make up your own mind about your children's education. Your children are your most precious asset. Americans have rightly resisted unconstitutional government for decades. Resistance to such interference is a defense of the Constitution, and of parents' biblical responsibilities. Home-school legal defense associations exist which, for a flat annual membership fee, will help defend home schoolers in court in case of state harassment.[32] These cases often are won on appeal. Local or state laws used to intimidate parents may be unconstitutional.

There are many possible options to explore for your child's education. We have endeavored to show what is being taught in public schools and how curriculums might be improved. We have presented some of the alternatives which many parents have taken. In conclusion, we want to emphasize once more that you are responsible for the children God has entrusted to you until they are ready to enter society. We hope you will join other parents who are determined to take charge of their children's education.

Footnotes

[1] Proverbs 22:6, KJV.

[2] Deuteronomy 6:6-7, KJV.

[3] "In the Search for a Comprehensive Educational Model," *Rebuilding American Education*, Martin Quam Press, 1979, p. 9.

[4] *Ibid.*, p. 7.

[5] Available from The Gablers, P.O. Box 7518, Longview, TX 75607. See Appendix 2 for ordering information.

[6] "The Bright Flight," *Newsweek*, April 20, 1981, p. 66.

[7] *Ibid.*

[8] *Ibid.*, p. 69.

[9] *Ibid.*, p. 68.

[10] *Ibid.*

[11] Christian school associations include: Association of Christian Schools International, Paul Kienel, Exec. Dir., P.O. Box 4097, Whittier, CA 90607; Christian Educators of the Southeast, A.A. Baker, Exec. Dir., 177 St. Cedd Ave., Pensacola, FL 32503; Maine Association of Christian Schools, Steven M. Hersey, Exec. Dir., 1476 Broadway, Bangor, ME 04401, American Association of Christian Schools, 10195 Main St., Suite P, P.O. Box 1088, Fairfax, VA 22030.

[12] Cited from manuscript of George Barna and William Paul McKay's *Vital Signs: Emerging Social Trends and the Future of American Christianity*, p. 8 in the chapter, "Divided We Stand, United We Fall: Educating the Next Generation of Christians," to be published by Crossway Books, 1984.

[13] "Christian Education: The Hope of Our Republic," Edward C.

Facey, pp. 61-65. *Journal of Christian Education*.
[14]Available from the Gablers, P.O. Box 7518, Longview, TX 75607.
[15]Sue Welch, "Counting the Cost," *Moody Monthly*, March 1984, pp. 26-30.
[16]John W. Whitehead, "Courting the Right," *Moody Monthly*, March 1984, pp. 22-24.
[17]Raymond and Dorothy Moore, *Home Grown Kids*, Word Books, 1981, pp. 226-227. Information available: Hewitt Research Foundation, Dr. Raymond Moore, President, P.O. Box 9, 36211 S.E. Sunset View, Washougal, WA 98671.
[18]*The Chattanooga Times*, August 10, 1984, p. B-1.
[19]*Pierce* v. *Society of Sisters*, 268 U.S. 510, 535, (1925) as cited in *Moody Monthly*, March 1984, p. 22. See also *Meyer v. Nebraska* (1925).
[20]*Wisconsin v. Yoder*, 406 U.S. 205, 232 (1972). Other Supreme Court statements favoring parental rights include: "It is cardinal with us that the custody, care and nurture of the child reside first in the parents, whose primary function and freedom include preparation for obligations the state can neither supply nor hinder." *Prince v. Massachusetts* 321 U.S. 158 166 (1943). See also *Abington v. Schempp*, 374 U.S. 203-302 (1963), and *Mercer v. Michigan*, 1974, as cited in vol. 43, *Law Weekly*, p. 3354.
[21]Raymond and Dorothy Moore, *Home Grown Kids*, Word Books, 1981, p. 24.
[22]*Ibid.*, pp. 23-24.
[23]Raymond Moore, "The School at Home," *Moody Monthly*, March 1984, pp. 18-20.
[24]*Ibid.*, p. 20.
[25]*Ibid.*, p. 19.
[26]Available from the Gablers, see footnote 5.
[27]Virginia Birt Baker, *Teaching Your Children at Home*, P.O. Box 1237, Quitman, TX 75783.
[28]*The Chattanooga Times*, August 10, 1984, p. B-1.
[29]Christian Liberty Academy, 203 East McDonald Rd., Prospect Heights, IL 60070.
[30]Welch, "Counting the Cost," *Moody Monthly*, March 1984, p. 27.
[31]*Ibid.*, p. 18.
[32]Home School Legal Defense Association, P.O. Box 2091, Washington, D.C. 20013, provides approximately 80 percent of defense costs to their members.

ACKNOWLEDGMENTS

Whatever our success in our twenty-four year battle for textbook reform, we know that "we have this treasure in earthen vessels, that the excellency of the power may be of God, and not of us" (2 Cor. 4:7). The credit goes to our precious Lord Jesus Christ, to whom we have confessed our sins, and received as Saviour; and who has promised, "I am the resurrection, and the life: he that believeth in Me, though he were dead, yet shall he live. And whosoever liveth and believeth in Me shall never die" (John 11:25-26). He also has promised, that "if God be for us, who can be against us?" (Rom. 8:31) We always face great opposition, but we are assured of ultimate success if we persevere in the struggle, and we have often found this true.

Spiritually speaking, we have all the help we need; but humanly speaking, we need all the help we can get. One of the benefits of textbook work is all the fine people we meet. We pray that they too will find Christ. But textbook reform rightly unites many Americans who disagree about much else, and who, despite their differences, work for the common good, for all our children must live in the society which textbooks will largely create.

MEL AND NORMA GABLER
JANUARY 1985

Get Expert Help Fast

We have the world's largest textbook review library, the most experience in all phases of textbook reviewing and state textbook-adoption procedures—and a small staff. We are glad to answer our mail as time permits, but please phone your urgent needs to assure quick attention. Among our thousands of quality printed forms are handbooks, textbook reviews, charts, and rating sheets.

Handbooks

Our handbooks are a gold mine of specialized information on the most common problem areas of curriculum and textbook reviewing. Some topics require two or more handbooks to cover the spectrum of available material. All handbooks are continuously updated with the most helpful facts, arguments, readings, and resources on their subjects. Our most popular handbooks include:

HB-1	Humanism		Private Schools)
HB-2	Values Clarification	HB-7	Drug Education
		HB-8	Death Education
HB-3A	Sex Education	HB-9	Phonics
HB-3B	Sex Education	HB-10	Creation Science
HB-3C	Sex Education	HB-12A	Home Schooling— General Information
HB-4	Acceptable Sex Education		
HB-5	Court Rulings Favoring Parental Rights	HB-12B	Home Schooling— Legislative and Legal Resources
HB-6	Acceptable Texts (Primarily for		

HB-13	MACOS (Man: A Course of Study	HB-23A	Dungeons and Dragons
HB-14	Censorship	HB-23B	Dungeons and Dragons
HB-15	Sensitivity Training	HB-24	Sources and Resources for Christian Schools
HB-16	Reality Therapy		
HB-18	Involvement Helps (Help in Getting Involved)	HB-27	Recommended Reading/Literature
HB-19	Textbook Ratings and Examples	HB-28	P.P.B.S. (Planned Program Budgeting Systems)
HB-20	Textbook Review Criteria and Examples	HB-29	Parenting and the PTA

Textbook Reviews

Our thousands of textbook reviews vary in length, author, and purpose. We have several reviews for many texts. A thorough review of one 500-page high school textbook takes about two weeks and thirty typewritten pages. Thus, our textbook review library can save you lots of time.

Our reviews can help you better word and structure your own reviews. But however extensive our reviews or however inexperienced you are, always read the textbooks yourself and write your own reviews, because:

Our reviews may be incomplete. Our reviews may have missed major defects in a text, or overlooked important passages which document them. Personal examination of a text always strengthens your case, and builds your confidence.

Our reviews may be obsolete. Textbook passages and/or page numbers referenced in our reviews may not correlate with the text version submitted in your state. Sometimes passages in later printings even of the same edition are changed, in response to complaints in earlier reviews. Skeptics will use one such discrepancy in the review you file, to discredit your whole participation in your state's textbook adoption process.

Secondhand information is worthless under cross-examination. Your review(s) will run the gauntlet of a panel of hostile critics.

Our predigested review(s) cannot give you the firsthand background information and personal knowledge of the text(s) to handle tough oral questions convincingly.

Charts
Our charts rank five textbooks on one subject and grade level (e.g., elementary Science, elementary Language Arts; eighth-grade Civics; high school World History). Each chart compares, in brief parallel columns, the texts' treatment of major topics of their subject. Each chart is always fully documented by careful reviews (available on request) representing hundreds or thousands of hours of quality time, and often by other information as well.

Rating Sheets
Our rating sheets rank two to four separate sets of textbooks, on different subject areas and grade levels. They do not themselves defend the rankings, but list the available charts and reviews which do.

Books
Textbooks on Trial by Dr. James C. Hefley (Victor Books). Tells how the Gablers got involved in textbook reviewing, and how you can too; called an outstanding book of the year it was published; available in hardback from the Gablers.

Are Textbooks Harming Your Children? by Dr. James C. Hefley (Mott Media). The paperback edition of *Textbooks on Trial*, with a fresh epilogue; available at your local Christian bookstore, or from the Gablers.

What Are They Teaching Our Children? by Mel and Norma Gabler (Victor Books). Explains current abuses in textbooks and how to correct them; available at your local Christian bookstore or from the Gablers.

Financial Policy
Our high quality printed materials are uniquely effective in adversarial situations like textbook and curriculum challenges. Our suggested minimum contributions cover their mailing and handling, not the real costs of providing them. We are a Christian faith mission, sustained wholly by God's provision through

those who care for the future of America's schoolchildren.

Address and Phone
THE MEL GABLERS
EDUCATIONAL RESEARCH ANALYSTS
P.O. BOX 7518
LONGVIEW, TEXAS 75607-7518
(214) 753-5993